THE SUICIDE
MAGNET

THE SUICIDE
MAGNET

Inside the Battle to Erect a Safety
Barrier on Toronto's Bloor Viaduct

PAUL McLAUGHLIN

DUNDURN
PRESS

Publisher: Kwame Scott Fraser | Acquiring editor: Russell Smith
Cover designer: Laura Boyle
Cover image: Peter MacCallum

Library and Archives Canada Cataloguing in Publication

Title: The suicide magnet : inside the battle to erect a safety barrier on Toronto's Bloor viaduct / Paul McLaughlin.
Names: McLaughlin, Paul, 1950- author.
Description: Includes index.
Identifiers: Canadiana (print) 20230473547 | Canadiana (ebook) 2023047358X | ISBN 9781459751408 (softcover) | ISBN 9781459751415 (PDF) | ISBN 9781459751422 (EPUB)
Subjects: LCSH: Suicide—Ontario—Toronto—Prevention—Citizen participation. | LCSH: Bridges—Ontario—Toronto—Safety measures.
Classification: LCC HV6548.C32 T67 2023 | DDC 362.2809713/541—dc23

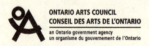

We acknowledge the support of the Canada Council for the Arts and the Ontario Arts Council for our publishing program. We also acknowledge the financial support of the Government of Ontario, through the Ontario Book Publishing Tax Credit and Ontario Creates, and the Government of Canada.

Dundurn Press
1382 Queen Street East
Toronto, Ontario, Canada M4L 1C9
dundurn.com, @dundurnpress 𝕐 f ⌾

To Al Birney and Michael McCamus,
who fought and won the good fight.

This was his first child and it had already become a murderer.
— Michael Ondaatje, *In the Skin of a Lion*

Contents

1

Bridge of Troubled Souls

I t's impossible to know what thirty-five-year-old Martin Kruze was thinking as he headed east on the subway out of downtown Toronto en route to the Broadview Avenue station on Thursday, October 30, 1997. Was he calm because of the decision he had made or was he tormented with anguish?

Broadview was the first stop after the train clacked across a platform built directly underneath the Prince Edward Viaduct in double-decker style. The massive five-arched steel-and-concrete structure, some 494 metres long (1,620 feet), spans the slender Don River, as well as its cavernous namesake valley below. A section of the heavily travelled vehicle route, the Don Valley Parkway, also winds down below.

Officially opened on October 18, 1918, the bridge united the west and east sides of the city by transportation and foot, a critical structure in the development of the burgeoning metropolis of some half a million people.

The original name was the Bloor Viaduct; a new moniker was proposed almost a year later following a three-day visit to Toronto by Edward, the Prince of Wales (who would later become King Edward VIII until his abdication in December 1936). The prince was immensely popular in Canada, especially because of his service in the British Army during the First World War, for which he had won the Military Cross. Shortly after his tour, the Toronto City Council asked if the city could name the bridge after him. He consented, and on October 6, 1919, it was officially christened the Prince Edward Viaduct, although his royal highness was not in attendance. The name never stuck, and almost all Torontonians call it the Bloor Viaduct or the Bloor Street Viaduct.

It was a majestic architectural accomplishment. Soon after its construction, however, a dark notoriety emerged: The bridge had become a "suicide magnet," a place that a small but significant number of people decided was a "romantic" public location from which to kill themselves. It's unlikely many who crossed over the bridge during their commute to work or shop knew it was second in North America only to the Golden Gate Bridge in San Francisco in total number of deaths from people jumping off it.

When Kruze emerged from the subway around 11:00 a.m., he was greeted by a delicious blast of sunshine and seasonable temperatures. A few minutes later, he walked to a spot on the south side of the viaduct. After climbing on top of the bridge's railing, he yelled, "Watch me!" to a couple of pedestrians passing by and plunged to his death, some forty metres (131 feet) to the Don Valley below.

What had triggered Kruze to end his life, some close to him believed, was the lenient sentence of two years less a day in prison a judge had imposed three days earlier on Gordon Stuckless, who had pleaded guilty to sexually assaulting more than two dozen boys at Maple Leaf Gardens over a period of about twenty years, including Kruze. "Martin was devastated," his sister-in-law, Teresa, later said. "It was a large slap in the face. It plunged him into such a deep despair. He felt broken."

But the real source of Kruze's despair was what had happened to him as a young teenager with dreams of becoming a National Hockey League player.

Kruze was one of the victims of a horrific pedophile ring that operated, seemingly with impunity, for many years at Maple Leaf Gardens, the legendary home of the Toronto Maple Leafs hockey team. He idolized the Leafs, as did so many boys.

A talented young hockey player in 1974, Kruze (who was then called Arnie; he changed it to Martin many years later), at age thirteen, had been introduced to George Hannah, the Leafs' equipment manager. They met through a contact of Arnie's father, Imants, whose curtain and drapery business supplied the Gardens. Imants had fought for the U.S. Army during the

Second World War, while his mother, Astrida, had come to Canada from Latvia at age twenty after Russia had invaded her county.

Hannah, about age fifty at the time, took an immediate shine to the angelic-looking teenager with white-blond bangs. He soon introduced Arnie to Gordon Stuckless, a twenty-five-year-old assistant equipment manager.

Hannah began bestowing gifts on the young boy, such as access to the press box during games, visits to the dressing room to meet the players, dinners at the arena's exclusive Hot Stove lounge, used sticks, and other treasured perks. He also dangled the intoxicating possibility of a tryout with the Toronto Marlies, the Leafs' American Hockey League team. Its illustrious alumni included George Armstrong, who was not long retired as the Leafs' respected captain. To an aspiring player, a chance to play on the Marlies, which was a very real stepping stone to the Leafs, was the ultimate seduction.

"[Hannah] made me feel like a king," Kruze wrote about the grooming process some twenty years later, "but what a price I paid."

Not long before Arnie turned fourteen, Hannah and Stuckless began sexually abusing the young teenager at the Gardens, known colloquially as Puckingham Palace. Constructed in late 1931, the aging building offered numerous small offices, rooms, dark hallways, and other locations where abuse could take place unobserved. The assaults continued for seven years, sometimes involving other employees in group sex activities, which permanently damaged Kruze. He said later that Hannah had "shattered" his love of life and that he often wanted to die during the horrible ordeals. "From thirteen to twenty years old, I would be in bed … and pray for God to take me. They robbed me of my innocence."

The abuse finally ended in 1982, but the years following were incredibly difficult for Arnie. He became addicted to drugs, alcohol, sex, and food, all-too-common consequences of what he had endured. He also attempted suicide on more than one occasion.

"It's a matter of public record that Martin tried to take his life several times in the past," broadcaster Teresa Kruze said after his death. She said her brother-in-law had frequently been "pulled" off the viaduct while contemplating killing himself.

Martin was fascinated with the viaduct, says Martin's brother, Gary, who was also an accomplished hockey player. "The very last Junior A hockey team I played for, the Dixie Beehives, one of our players, Dan, had jumped off the Bloor Viaduct." Martin often came to Gary's games and knew about the suicide.

"He'd mention Dan a lot, and he almost had an obsession about [what had happened]," Gary says. "For about ten years after that, when he was in a bad way or depressed or something — we didn't know why, at that time — he threatened to jump off that bridge many times. I'd say, 'Oh, Martin, come on, you're not gonna jump off the bridge, come on, come on, what's wrong?'"

The Kruze family desperately tried to get Martin the help he needed. "He was constantly getting therapy and going in and out of places like the Donwood [Institute, a public hospital for addiction]. He was constantly trying to get help, but it was just such a struggle," says Gary.

Martin's second-last suicide attempt occurred at a different city bridge six days before he leapt from the Bloor Viaduct. Only the timely intervention by a police constable stopped him from jumping. He was taken to Toronto East General Hospital but was soon released, against the wishes of his family. Martin's family tried to get him admitted to Toronto Western Hospital in the days leading up to his final suicide attempt but couldn't. The psychiatrist there would not admit him, saying that Martin would not "act it out."

The unwillingness, or inability, of hospitals to keep suicidal persons under their control was a common complaint of many families with a loved one dealing with mental health issues during the 1990s.

Kruze Takes Action

In 1992, when he was thirty years old and struggling greatly with his anguish, Kruze telephoned Maple Leaf Gardens and told the person on the other end of the line what Hannah (who had died in 1984) and Stuckless had done to him and numerous other boys. He also identified long-term usher, John Paul Roby, as another abuser. The person Kruze spoke to noted that similar complaints had already been lodged against the men.

In 1989, Toronto businessman Tom Bingham, the father of another abuse survivor, learned that Stuckless, who had been convicted of sexually abusing his thirteen-year-old son two years earlier and spent some time in jail as a result, was still working at the Gardens.

"He wrote a letter to Donald Giffin, a longtime Gardens director who became president following [owner Harold] Ballard's death [in 1990]," *Maclean's* reported in 1997. "In no uncertain terms, Bingham warned Giffin that Stuckless was a convicted pedophile. Gardens officials then asked Stuckless to leave the Gardens. Bingham told *Maclean's* that he was far from satisfied when he received a reply from Gardens officials that simply thanked him for his correspondence. 'I wish they had gone to the police,' said Bingham. 'Instead, they told me that Stuckless had paid his debt to society.'"

SMALL RECOMPENSE

Toronto lawyer Susan Vella represented Martin Kruze in a lawsuit against Maple Leaf Gardens. After the organization declined to accept a million-dollar offer in 1993, Vella filed a $1.75 million claim with the Ontario Court of Justice.

Negotiations resumed but moved slowly. In August 1995, the Leafs offered $25,000; Vella understandably wanted to turn it down but "the suit was taking such a toll on Kruze that both lawyer and the client believed it needed to be brought to a conclusion as soon as possible," Cathy Vine and Paul Challen wrote in their 2002 book, *Gardens of Shame: The Tragedy of Martin Kruze and the Sexual Abuse at Maple Leaf Gardens*.

Vella countered with $60,000 and the team accepted. To obtain the money, Kruze had to sign a non-disclosure agreement (NDA).

A few months earlier, the Ontario Criminal Injuries Compensation Board awarded Kruze $17,000 plus $500 for legal costs.

A highly respected litigator with Rochon Genova, Vella was appointed a judge of the Superior Court of Justice of Ontario in 2020.

Years later, Maple Leaf President Cliff Fletcher would claim that the failure to involve police was because Kruze wanted to remain anonymous and had been pursuing a civil settlement rather than criminal charges.

It took until January 1997 before Kruze, who would become an advocate for victims of sexual abuse, disregarded the NDA he'd signed upon accepting a sixty-thousand-dollar settlement from the Leafs and contacted the Toronto police; he told them everything that had happened to him. In February, Stuckless and Roby were arrested and charged for their crimes, which Detective Dave Tredrea said were "common knowledge among the [Gardens] staff."

Another victim, John McCarthy, said that "Harold Ballard, the Gardens' autocratic owner from 1971 until his death in 1990, would often walk by as Hannah and a group of kids sat watching TV together — or were coming out of the team sauna naked," *Maclean's* reported. "Even though the teens had no particular reason for being in the building, no one in charge asked any questions."

In *Gardens of Shame*, the authors, Cathy Vine and Paul Challen, went even further. "Many of the survivors interviewed for this book believe that the Gardens management knew what [Hannah, Stuckless, and Roby] were doing there but did nothing to stop it," they wrote. "Several … also claim that Gardens officials — including Harold Ballard — actually witnessed acts of sexual abuse taking place in offices and the stands but did nothing to stop them."

One survivor, Brian Silber, "has at least one image locked in his mind that haunts him to this day: being abused [by Stuckless] in front of Harold Ballard's desk, while Ballard sat behind it," they reported.

In October 2002, a lawsuit against Maple Leaf Gardens included an allegation by a victim referred to as R.L. that Ballard had once sexually propositioned him. "Ballard apparently asked my client to lick ice cream off his penis," R.L.'s lawyer, Loretta Merritt, told the *Globe and Mail*.

Merritt, a partner in the Toronto firm Torkin Manes, where her practice focuses on civil sexual assault cases, says she had witnesses who "can back up that Ballard knew [about the abuses]."

A Deadly Prank

As a result of Kruze's highly publicized death, questions about the location he chose for his death were starting to be asked. Media reports brought out the startling information that three hundred or more people had, at that point, selected the Bloor Viaduct as the location for their suicides. The number would ultimately increase to about four hundred before the barrier was installed.

Then another widely reported suicide stoked the conversation even more.

On December 10, 1997, the principal of St. Michael's Choir School called six students to his office. The prestigious school, which was located not far from the Eaton Centre shopping complex in downtown Toronto, boasted several notable alumni, including *Les Misérables* star Michael Burgess and Scottish Canadian tenor John McDermott, famous for his rendering of "Danny Boy."

The principal confronted the nervous group, which included seventeen-year-old Kenneth Au Yeung, a straight-A grade twelve student, about an entry in the school yearbook they had all worked on. The students had jokingly, and falsely, written that a certain teacher was "a former equipment manager at Maple Leaf Gardens," a reference to the recently exposed sexual abuse scandal. "[The yearbook committee] thought they had deleted the file," Au Yeung's mother, Catherine, would later say. "[Kenneth] was concerned that being part of the six, his reputation would be ruined," and that he'd never be accepted at a university.

The next day, the school brought in an off-duty police officer, thirty-six-year-old Constable Christopher Downer, a seventeen-year veteran of the Toronto police force and "a former choir-school boy who for years had served as something between friendly neighborhood police officer and the school's private bouncer," *Maclean's* reported.

Downer confronted the students, threatening that unless someone confessed to the potentially libellous publication, they could all face criminal charges. Au Yeung and another student owned up to co-authorship of the piece, although Au Yeung had been on holidays with his family when the final editing of the yearbook, which mistakenly included the impish comment, was conducted.

A few hours later, as a light snow wafted down on the city, Au Yeung walked some three kilometres (just under two miles) northeast to the Bloor Viaduct. At 12:20 p.m., according to twenty-five-year-old Chantelle Gobeil, who was driving west across the bridge, Au Yeung put his hands on the stone railing and hurtled over it, "as if hopping a fence." The police later said he had left a suicide note in his coat pocket that simply read: "Sorry for everything."

Maclean's later reported that "a new page was pasted in [the yearbook] and the book [was] sent back out to students. The financial cost to fix the error was a couple of hundred dollars. The real cost may never be known."

Au Yeung's death was a suspected "copycat suicide," because of the reference to the Maple Leaf Gardens scandal. This seemed to be confirmed by his mother in a letter of memorial she distributed to friends and family prior to the funeral, which the *Star* subsequently published.

"I still remember the day recently when we drove under the Bloor Street Viaduct on the way to mass and we discussed the deaths that had occurred there and how I markedly said to him, 'You of course would never do a thing like that.' And he answered flippantly, 'Of course not.' I went on to say there are no problems in life that cannot be solved. He obviously was too muddled and stressed to remember our conversation. He took things very seriously, probably more so than most teenagers the school is accustomed to."

While most suicides are voluntarily not reported by the media for fear of inspiring copycats, that rule is sidestepped in high-profile public cases such as those involving Kruze and Au Yeung. Numerous media stories addressed the circumstances that led to their deaths and their choice of the viaduct as the place to die. On December 9, for example, the *Toronto Star* ran an article entitled "Bridge of Troubled Souls," about the small but growing movement to "fence the Bloor Viaduct for safety."

The viaduct's infamy as a "bridge of death," as it was starting to be called, escalated in early 1998 following a third widely reported event. On February 19, forty-six-year-old Jim Pridmore jumped to his death, causing two lanes of the Don Valley Parkway to be closed during the always busy morning rush hour.

Some hours earlier, Pridmore had murdered a woman he had been having a longtime affair with, forty-five-year-old Jessica Romano, and left her bloodied body in the front seat of her car. Apparently, he was separating from his wife and believed Romano was leaving the man she lived with so they could be together. When he found out she had changed her mind, his heartbreak and anger drove him to kill her and himself.

Pridmore's nephew, Michael, said in an interview that Jim, who worked as a printer, had written a love poem for Romano and entered it in a newspaper contest. That surprised Michael: "[Jim] was never really poetic."

Among those disturbed by the alarming suicides at the viaduct was Toronto police superintendent Aidan Maher. He had previously commanded two of the three Toronto police divisions that had jurisdiction over the bridge. In 1986, he had written to the Metropolitan Toronto Council and the regional coroner of Toronto advocating that a barrier be erected after a fourteen-year-old boy, a friend of his daughter, had jumped off the viaduct but had survived.

Noting that some jumpers land on cars travelling on the Bayview Extension or the Don Valley Parkway, he said when this happens it can cause accidents, sometimes seriously injuring drivers and passengers. "It's not a pretty sight."

Many people disagreed that a barrier needed to be built. A prevailing response was that a barrier would only send a suicidal person to another location or find another means of ending their life. During a local radio phone-in program just after Kruze's death, newly elected mayor Mel Lastman was asked if he supported an anti-suicide fence on the viaduct. "I understand the problem of depression. I don't have it," he said, somewhat hesitantly. "I don't feel good about people committing suicide. But putting a fence around the bridge, I'm not sure if that is the solution."

Lastman's position did not sit well with two men, both ordinary Toronto citizens, who each had personal and traumatic reasons to care deeply about the role the viaduct played in the number of suicides in the city. Al Birney, a retired salesman blessed with the gift of the gab, and Michael McCamus, a twenty-six-year-old student in the journalism certificate program at Ryerson Polytechnic University, as it was then named, had come together earlier that year, on their own time and money, to lobby city council into recognizing the viaduct as a suicide magnet and, as a result, into voting to erect a barrier.

They believed fervently there was compelling evidence that would easily convince the politicians to act and to do so quickly. Their nascent campaign, however, had so far mostly fallen on deaf ears.

"Although suicide can seem like something depressing to talk about," says McCamus, "from the outset Al and I tried to emphasize hope and optimism. We believed that if a barrier was built, some people — not all, granted — would seek treatment or some other solution because the 'magnet' was no longer accessible. Many studies had shown this to be true, but it wasn't an easy message to get across most of the time, at least when we started our campaign."

The attention generated by the prominent suicides, they now hoped, would be the leverage they required to persuade city hall of the urgent need to fund a barrier.

But that's rarely how things work at city hall. Little did Birney, McCamus, and the rest of the volunteers who worked with them realize it would take almost six years to accomplish their goal, nor how much the cost of a barrier would balloon during that time, and, more importantly, how many people would die unnecessarily as an endless debate played out.

2

A Monument to Progress and Despair

The story of the Bloor Street Viaduct can't be told without saluting Roland Caldwell Harris — "Roly" to friends; R.C. in official documents — who was one of Toronto's, and likely Canada's, greatest city builders. Born in 1875 in what is now called North York, Ontario, he spent a brief time as a cub reporter before joining the local civil service in 1899. By 1912, the high school graduate had showcased such leadership talent and work ethic that he was appointed Toronto's first Commissioner of Public Works, a position he retained until he died of a heart attack in 1945.

"[Harris] left his civic fingerprints all over Toronto, building hundreds of kilometres of sidewalks, sewers, paved roads, streetcar tracks, public baths and washrooms, landmark bridges, and even the precursor plans to the GO commuter rail network," a 2012 article in the *Globe and Mail* noted. Dalhousie University architecture professor Steve Mannell, who has studied Harris's career added: "The significance of Harris a hundred years later is that we're still living fundamentally in the city he imagined."

A visionary and reformer, the portly Harris, who eschewed the limelight, began his career during a time when Toronto's population was growing at a spectacular rate. From just under 210,000 in 1901, it had swelled to 381,000 ten years later, an increase of 83 percent. By the end of the second decade, the population was more than 410,000.

Although he had numerous significant accomplishments, Harris is best remembered for two iconic structures. Likely because of its eponymous name, the one most associated with the cigar-loving public servant is the spectacular R.C. Harris Water Treatment Plant, located in southeast Toronto. To this day, it provides about 30 percent of the city's drinking water, a testament to Harris's determination to modernize the city's water treatment system.

"This palatial Art-Deco building looks like a museum," Atlas Obscura Online observed in 2009. "Surprisingly, the inside of the building is similarly elegant, with cavernous halls and marble passages, all full of filtration equipment. This opulence has earned the building the nickname 'Palace of Purification.'"

Commemorated on a 2011 Canada Post stamp honouring Canada's five most dazzling art-deco edifices, the plant, a sprawling multi-building site, sits grandly on the north shore of Lake Ontario, offering its numerous visitors a sweeping view of the Great Lake.

It's much less known that Harris was also the driving force behind the construction of the Bloor Street Viaduct, a bold and critically important architectural feat that directly helped bridge Toronto's soon-to-burgeon east end with the city centre.

The idea for the viaduct preceded Harris. "Plans to build the bridge emerged as early as 1897," Ann Marie F. Murnaghan, an assistant professor of humanities at York University, wrote in *The City, the Country, and Toronto's Bloor Viaduct, 1897–1919*. The embryonic concept gained support on August 25, 1910, when American consulting engineers Jacob and Davies recommended a city-wide network of "tubes" (as subways were then called) to reduce Toronto's traffic congestion. It was an ambitious plan that included the first proposal of "a double-decked Viaduct to connect Bloor St. with Danforth Ave."

The report, which had been commissioned by city council for five thousand dollars, became the centrepiece of Controller Horatio Hocken's 1910 mayoral campaign, his election posters proclaiming, "Hocken for Mayor. Tubes for the People." But voters were not ready for Hocken's visionary leadership, nor the staggering $23 million cost of Jacob and Davies's imagined tubes. Hocken lost the New Year's Day election of 1910.

Almost three years later, on October 21, 1912, Hocken pulled off a political comeback when city council elected him to succeed outgoing mayor

George Geary. Under Hocken, R.C. Harris began revising the tubes-and-viaduct proposal. Repeated efforts to fund the bridge, however, were rejected by voters in three referenda (all held on January 1, in 1910, 1911, and 1912, when it lost by fifty-nine votes).

An influential body that opposed the bridge was the Guild of Civic Art, a collection of architects, town planners, artists, and other citizens concerned about the protection of nature in the city, among other mandates. The guild believed a viaduct, in the design that had been proposed (a straight east-west line), would destroy the natural beauty of the area, especially the scenic Rosedale Ravine, which would be severely impacted by such an imposing undertaking. Local residents, meanwhile, dubbed the concept "the bridge to nowhere," due to the small population in Toronto east at the time.

Ironically, a member of the guild, architect John Lyle, devised a solution: a landfill terrace that would extend the southeast end of Bloor Street (at the western starting point), allowing the bridge to traverse the Don Valley without destroying the ravine. His plan, which was endorsed by R.C. Harris, was approved by voters in a 1913 referendum by more than nine thousand votes. A budget was set at $2.5 million (an equivalent of about $66 million today).

Harris oversaw the viaduct's construction, working in tandem with Edmund Burke, the lead designer of the architectural component, and Thomas Taylor, the designing and construction engineer. Burke was one of Canada's most accomplished architects (his numerous achievements included the Robert Simpson Company building, known as Simpson's, in downtown Toronto). Working with a team of engineers, Burke devised a three-section structure: the Don, 494 metres (1,620 feet) long, which crossed over the Don River valley and had five main steel-and-concrete beaux-arts style arches; the Rosedale, which skirted over the Rosedale Ravine; and the Bloor, which began on the enhanced embankment along the edge of the Rosedale Ravine. In total, the viaduct would stretch just under four metres (thirteen feet) short of one and a half kilometres (one mile) in length.

At the urging of Hocken, and with the full support of Harris, Burke, following the Jacob and Davies 1910 recommendation, left open spaces in the Viaduct's columns beneath the roadway that could accommodate the weight of subway trains in the future.

Hocken was a fervent social reformer whose many accomplishments included a program to distribute free milk to children living in slums. His support for the Jacob-Davies prescient proposal for the city's future transportation needs saved taxpayers an incredible amount of money many years later; the Bloor-Danforth subway line that operates underneath the viaduct wasn't opened until 1966. It's impossible to fathom the cost of adding a subway platform to the viaduct, if at all doable, some fifty years after it had been built.

Throughout the design process, Harris made certain the viaduct met both practical and aesthetic standards. "Unlike his [public works] predecessors, [Harris] insisted on high architectural and landscaping quality in the design of his works projects," Christopher Hume, the architecture critic for the *Toronto Star* wrote in November 2002. "He regarded structures such as the St. Clair Reservoir built in the late 1920s, in both aesthetic and functional terms." Known as "the other palace of water," the reservoir, which featured limestone and yellow brick and was topped by a public park, was another Harris-directed initiative (both water plants were designed by Scottish-born architect Thomas Pomphrey).

Construction of the challenging viaduct project began in January 1915, thanks largely to "a small army of immigrant workers," according to the City of Toronto document "100th Anniversary of the Bloor Viaduct." Mayor Tommy Church turned the first sod on the sixteenth of the month. A future member of Parliament, it was said Church "never met a hand he wouldn't shake." *Toronto Daily Star* reporter Ernest Hemingway poked fun at this trait when he covered a boxing match Church attended. "The mayor enjoyed the first bout hugely," the future novelist observed. "During it he shook hands with everyone around him. He did not seem to know when the bout stopped, as he was still shaking hands when the bell rang for the end of the last round."

In an era when municipal politicians were elected to one-year terms, Church was returned to his office a record seven consecutive times, despite considerable negative press from Hemingway. When he died in 1950, his public funeral was the largest in Toronto's history, according to a 2014 *Toronto Star* article.

The engineering component of the bridge was an unprecedented challenge, archivist Anastasia Rodgers wrote in her 2002 case study, "Constructing Beauty: The Photographs Documenting the Construction of the Bloor Viaduct." Thankfully, head engineer James Hodges commissioned Scottish-born William Notman, the first Canadian photographer to have an international reputation, to record the years-long undertaking. "The result is a series of photographs that not only illustrate the various phases of construction, including the building of the cofferdams and masonry piers, the staging for the erection of the superstructure, and its assembly from ironwork prefabricated in England, but also testify to human invention and artistry."

York University professor Murnaghan described the bridge as "an engineering feat spanning three valleys, making east-west travel in the growing city more efficient, improving the transportation of food and lumber. Symbolically, this monument highlighted the ability to overcome nature with a bridge and bring an aestheticized nature to the city. This contradiction

Close to completion.

between overcoming and improving access to nature is built into the bridge's planning and construction history."

In the Skin of a Pandemic

Many years later, when the viaduct was likely taken for granted by the thousands of people who used it daily, Sri Lankan–born Canadian writer Michael Ondaatje would also perceive its symbolic importance. "The Bridge" was the title of the second chapter of his 1987 novel, *In the Skin of a Lion*. The viaduct featured prominently in the book, as did the R.C. Harris Water Treatment Plant.

"Before the real city could be seen, it had to be imagined," Ondaatje wrote. "The bridge goes up in a dream. It will link the east end with the centre of the city. It will carry traffic, water, and electricity across the Don Valley. It will carry trains that have not even been invented yet. Men in a maze of wooden planks climb deep into the shattered light of blonde wood. A man is an extension of hammer, drill and fire. Drill smoke in his hair. A cap falls into the valley, gloves are buried in stone dust."

The building of the viaduct, which took four and one-half years in total, "was completed using elaborate wooden cranes, steam engines, winches and pulleys, and hand labour because modern hydraulic machines were not yet widely available. The work continued through World War I, when both men and materials were in short supply," according to a Toronto Public Library website. It was an incredible accomplishment, featuring six lanes for traffic.

One of the most significant infrastructure projects in Toronto's history, the viaduct was officially opened on October 18, 1918, upon the completion of the Don and Rosedale sections. About a month later, the first streetcar crossed the bridge. The Bloor section, however, "was still settling, and its opening was delayed until August 23, 1919," according to another City of Toronto document, "Bridging the Don: The Viaduct Opens." On that day, the viaduct became fully accessible to traffic.

Despite being an auspicious occasion, the 1918 ceremony to mark the formal ribbon-cutting was a low-key event. The official opening attracted

Streetcars connect west and east Toronto.

Mayor Tommy Church officially opens the viaduct, October 18, 1918.

little attention from the public or the press. The *Toronto Daily Star*, for example, ran a picture of the ceremony on the front page but no copy accompanied it.

There were two reasons for the muted response to such an important moment in the city's history: The First World War was almost at an end, the newspapers were focused on news of the war and the terrible number of Canadian casualties (more than sixty-five thousand), and the virulent Spanish influenza was rampaging through the city. One absent victim of the flu was Thomas Taylor, who had led the team of designers of the viaduct in his position at the Works department.

"Only a small number of officials joined the few spectators who had arrived to witness the ceremonies," noted "Bridging the Don." Before the fourth speaker had concluded his remarks, "the mayor, Tommy Church, called an abrupt halt to the ceremonies. 'We will not have any more speakers for, if we keep you any longer, we will be violating the Medical Officer's regulations as to gatherings of people.'"

Although the official launch may have been inauspicious, the viaduct was a huge success, warmly embraced by residents living east of the Don River. It was also lauded for what Rodgers called its "beauty and grandeur" that to some "borders on the romantic."

It is that romantic aura, unfortunately, that has contributed to the bridge's reputation as a suicide magnet. To some distressed people, the viaduct, which was easy to access, seemed to have a special allure, as if it offered a meaningful place to die.

In his novel, Ondaatje deployed a strand of magical realism to portray the bridge's dark underbelly. He imagined a nun who got lost and ended up walking, unsafely, on the structure: "The worst, the incredible had happened. A nun had fallen off the Prince Edward Viaduct before it was even finished. The men covered in wood shavings or granite dust held the women against them. And Commissioner Harris" — who was a character in the book — "at the far end stared along the mad pathway. This was his first child and it had already become a murderer."

The nun doesn't die — she is saved by a Macedonian labourer, Nicholas Temelcoff, a real-life character who somehow grabs her as she plummets

An impressive span.

downward. Ondaatje, who learned about Temelcoff at the Multicultural History Society, wrote that "he is famous on the bridge, a daredevil. He is given all the difficult jobs and he takes them. He descends into the air with no fear. He is a solitary. He assembles ropes, brushes the tackle and pulley at his waist, and falls off the bridge like a diver over the edge of a boat." But there's no denying the message the author chose to send: This magnificent structure had a sinister side to it, as if it was reminiscent of Jekyll and Hyde.

The viaduct's dark side was on Al Birney's mind in 2001 when he stood on the windy structure for an interview. The long-term lobbyist for a suicide barrier, who looked like the actor Karl Malden minus the bulbous nose, was taking part in a TVO documentary, *Never Coming Back*, that aired in May of that year.

"This bridge to me represents death," he said. "The bridge has been here for eighty-one years, and during those years over four hundred people have jumped. If you look right down there, you'll find among the garbage cans and the pop bottles, newspapers and old clothing is where [all those] people spent the last moments of their lives on Earth."

It's unlikely Birney was aware that the viaduct had a previous death toll, one from the years before it opened: Eighteen people working on the bridge had fallen to their death during construction.

Little is known about the labourers, with the exception of Temelcoff; Ondaatje once suggested the bridge be named after him.

There was no impetus to rename the viaduct at that time; but there was a period of years when a small number of citizens would fight to end its sinister allure to those struggling with their mental health. They would eventually win, but it would first require them to convince the city's politicians that suicide magnets actually exist.

TRAFFIC THEN AND NOW

On October 24, 1918, the *Toronto Daily Star* reported that "a city official made a count of cars passing over the new Bloor Viaduct between eight and nine o'clock at night, and counted 106 motor vehicles in twelve minutes, or at the rate of 530 per hour."

On October 11, 2003, while reporting on road closures on the viaduct to accommodate filming of *Resident Evil: Apocalypse*, the *Toronto Star* noted, "A May 2001 survey counted nearly 18,000 vehicles crossing between 6 a.m. and 6 p.m. on a typical weekday. Traffic will be forced to detour around the Viaduct tomorrow and Monday to allow the filming of explosive scenes for the movie, inconveniencing up to 20,000 residents and businesses."

3

An Unlikely Duo

I n early June 1997, former federal finance minister Michael Wilson, a powerful figure in Prime Minister Brian Mulroney's Conservative government until he retired from the Cabinet in 1993, addressed a local chapter of the Schizophrenia Society of Ontario (SSO), a volunteer organization of families of people with mental illnesses, in a labour union hall in Scarborough, Ontario. The fifty-nine-year-old Wilson was normally a reticent man. "His public speaking style could best be described as functional and effective, so long as the objective was to deliver a sober message in steady tones," Terence Corcoran once wrote in the *Financial Post*. "No audience ever roared and jumped or cheered wildly in the wake of a Michael Wilson speech." But now Wilson was to deliver an impassioned message, the tenor of which he had avoided during his long political career.

Wilson's presentation to the Scarborough SSO had nothing to do with politics or the economy — it was about his son, Cameron, who had died by suicide on April 24, 1995, at age twenty-nine. About five months before his death, Cameron had telephoned his father, who lived in the suburbs of Toronto, at 3:00 a.m. "You gotta come down, Dad!" Cameron pleaded. "You gotta come down right now!"

Frantically rushing to get dressed and into their car, Wilson and his wife, Margie, found their son after an agonizing search near his apartment in downtown Toronto. Cameron was "walking down the middle of the road, barefoot in the cold night air, dressed only in his pyjamas,"

Wilson wrote in his autobiography, *Something Within Me: A Personal and Political Memoir*.

He and Margie took their son to the Clarke Institute of Psychiatry (now the Centre for Addiction and Mental Health), where Wilson had volunteered in various capacities since he'd retired from politics. Cameron was treated for a "psychosis that left him confused and incoherent."

Cameron, who had worked for a while at National Trust, where his grandfather had served as president and a director, suffered from severe depression, likely due to having been sexually abused when he was twelve years old. "He struggled with the illness — his behaviour became erratic, he was fired from his job [for physically assaulting his boss] and was institutionalized for psychiatric care — but begged his family to not tell anyone for fear it would destroy his career prospects and scare away his friends," André Picard, health writer for the *Globe and Mail*, wrote some years later.

Cameron's concerns were all too common. In the mid-1990s, admitting to mental health problems had an unwanted stigma, although that has lessened to a degree in recent years.

After a suicide attempt, Cameron's parents took him back to the Clarke Institute. Their son again begged them not to reveal that he was being treated at a psychiatric hospital. "The depth of his fear of being spurned by society due to his illness — a condition that should have generated sympathy and support, not rejection — has never left me. It never will," Wilson wrote.

A few months later, Cameron killed himself by an undisclosed method. "He chose to take his life primarily because of an inability to deal with society's opinion of him as a mental health patient," Wilson wrote. "He feared, with some justification, the assumptions that his friends and the rest of society might make — that he was weak, that he craved attention, that he just needed to 'Snap out of it!'"

At Cameron's funeral, held at St. Clement's Anglican Church in Toronto, Michael Wilson decided in his eulogy to go public with the details of his son's illness. That determination led him to the SSO union hall some two years later, as part of his ongoing commitment to sharing his family's story — and his understanding of the causes and stigmas associated with mental illness. At the Clarke Institute, Wilson had learned that "mental illnesses are generally the result of an interplay of factors that include temperament, genetic makeup, hormones, and chemistry." It was nothing to be ashamed of, he told the receptive audience that evening in Scarborough.

A Near-Death Event

One person listening attentively was twenty-six-year-old Michael McCamus, a red-haired, plump-faced student who was pursuing a certificate in journalism while supporting himself by working at McDonald's.

McCamus, who possesses an almost eidetic memory, attended the speech, along with his father, Walter, his mother, Ruth, and his younger brother, Peter, at Michael's insistence. He wanted them to hear what Wilson had to share, because of Walter's history.

Michael's father had first been diagnosed with a mental illness in the early 1950s, when in his twenties. When Walter married Ruth in 1968, he had a blue-collar job making paint and paint products; Ruth was a head nurse at the Hospital for Sick Children, and also taught nursing at what was then called Ryerson Polytechnic Institute. In 1974, after Peter was born, Walter quit his job to become a stay-at-home husband. Michael says he and Peter had a rather normal and even idyllic childhood, until Michael's eighth year.

In the summer of 1979, Walter had what psychiatrists call a psychotic break — he was detached from reality. He had powerful paranoid delusions and believed people were plotting against him and his family and that he was in jeopardy. Walter saw a psychiatrist and was prescribed antipsychotic medications, which he would occasionally stop taking. He didn't like the side effects, which included feelings of mental slowness and lethargy. He couldn't relax. He was constantly folding and unfolding his arms, crossing and uncrossing his legs.

Matters escalated to an almost fatal degree in December 1981. The family had visited relatives in Midland, Ontario, near Georgian Bay, for Christmas dinner with Ruth's aunt and uncle, who functioned as if they were Michael and Peter's maternal grandparents. Walter had another psychotic episode after the meal and was pacing the halls of the house, ranting and raving about horrible, paranoid things that could happen to everyone.

The McCamuses left about 10:00 p.m. that night; it was bitterly cold, with ice and blowing snow making the roads treacherous.

Walter drove the family along a barely lit two-lane highway, toward Barrie, on their way south to Toronto. Somewhere between Midland and Barrie, Walter deliberately crossed the centre line, veering into oncoming traffic, resulting in a head-on collision between the McCamuses' car and a vehicle occupied by a retired couple.

Michael remembers a flash of lights and his mother screaming, "Walter, look out!" followed by a loud crash and all the car's windows shattering, as the family car was crushed like an accordion. Michael woke up in the mangled wreckage. "My father was hunched over the steering wheel; the entire driver's side was pressed into his chest," he says. "A good Samaritan stopped and led my mother, my brother, and me to her warm car. I saw the police and firefighters arrive. I could see both destroyed cars in the middle of the highway. They had to cut our car open to get my father out.

"My brother and I had some small cuts on our arms and face. On that night, Peter started talking in his sleep. He's been doing it ever since. My mother had a very sore neck, but not whiplash. We would learn later that my father had a fractured hip, which required surgery to repair, several broken ribs, and a punctured lung. The couple in the other car had injuries but, thankfully, survived. Somehow, my father didn't lose his driver's licence. His suicide attempt was well disguised as a car accident."

Walter was held involuntarily at Sunnybrook Hospital in Toronto following the "accident," as it had been ruled. He took antipsychotic medication every day and was released after a few weeks; he remained on the medication for decades.

"I need people to know that my father was not an evil man or an attempted murderer," Michael says many years later. "He was a good man, a devoted father, and a loyal husband. But he was severely, profoundly ill the night of the car accident. His mind had been assaulted by uncontrollable paranoid fears and a completely mangled perception of reality. He was not in control of his actions, nor were they the 'choices' of the thoughtful, sensitive, kindhearted person my dad was throughout his life. They were the actions of a person overpowered by unbearable fear and total loss of impulse control. People who have never experienced mental illness or never had a family member who suffered from it might find that difficult or impossible to understand, but it's absolutely true."

His father's fragile psychological makeup, the result of his schizophrenia, was the impetus behind Michael's insistence that the entire family attend Wilson's speech.

"I can't tell you how meaningful his speech at the SSO that night was to me," says McCamus. "I'm sure it made many people feel like they were not alone anymore, and that people in high places would not only listen to us, but would understand what we were going through, because they had experienced tragedy also."

Although it was inspiring to have the former finance minister candidly reveal his son's struggles, his speaking style remained somewhat plodding. "The speech was long, and by the end of it, the audience was getting tired and listless," McCamus says. "Then this older guy with thinning grey hair and piercing blue eyes started talking in an Irish accent. People sat up and listened. I was captivated. The audience was, too."

You Can Call Me Al

The older guy was sixty-seven-year-old John Albert (Al) Birney, a retired door-to-door salesman who ran event planning and publicity for the Scarborough chapter of the Schizophrenia Society of Ontario. He was born in the town of Lisnaskea, in County Fermanagh, Northern Ireland, where his family operated a grocery store called Birney's. "Our family is what you call Scots-Irish," his son, Mitch, says. His father had a licence plate sticker in Toronto that read, "I love Fermanagh."

When he was in his early twenties, Al met Kathleen Mitchell at a dance in Portrush, a small seaside Irish town. "I was born in Coagh, not far from where Al was born. It's so small it's not even on the map," she says. "We were both interested in dancing and carrying on, that type of thing."

At the dance Al told Kathleen, who was nineteen, she thinks, and three years younger than him, that he wanted to immigrate to Canada to explore new opportunities. "Would you like to come?" he asked. She said yes but she had no money. He told her he'd get a job after he arrived and would send money for a plane ticket.

After Al arrived in Toronto in the early 1950s and "moved in with an auntie," Kathleen says he found work (she thinks it had to do with engines) at Malton Airport (now Pearson International). True to his word, he sent her airfare. She flew to Canada on a 737. She, too, found a job at the airport. They were married soon after, in 1953, at a friend's home in Scarborough.

Al Birney possessed the blarney, which he put to great use as a salesman and, later, in the suicide-barrier campaign. "Al collected all kinds of stories, anecdotes, and jokes to share with anyone he encountered," a childhood friend remembers. "He was a storyteller and a joke teller, and a lot of fun to be around." He especially relished telling people they could call him Al, a riff on Paul Simon's 1986 hit from the *Graceland* album. "Everybody who met my father seemed to come away happier," says Mitch, age sixty-six, who owns the Fun in the Sun Ice Cream Parlour in Southampton, Ontario.

Al Birney began his SSO address by urging the audience to support an effort to "get a fence on the Bloor Street Viaduct," where so many people had jumped to their death. His request was not a random plea to help a generic mental health initiative; it was the essential component of a personal crusade born out of his own family crisis.

Al and his wife Kathleen had three children, one of whom, John Charles, was named after his father. Born in 1959, John had inherited Al's sense of humour, outgoing nature, and gift for oratory. In the early 1980s, however, John began acting strangely. The young man, who had begun a career as a successful salesman, became uncharacteristically moody, distant, and suspicious. His work and friendships suffered. His memory and concentration started to fail.

The family later learned that his mind had become overwhelmed with powerful paranoid thoughts of people watching him and following his every move. He had delusions of grandeur, of being on a secret messianic mission to save the world. He spent money impulsively and irrationally, once purchasing twelve wristwatches in one day.

John was eventually diagnosed with schizophrenia. Al and Kathleen were shocked and kept his diagnosis a secret, for fear their son would be misunderstood or stigmatized. To them, at the time, schizophrenia was the domain of madmen in lunatic asylums with multiple personalities and bizarre, outlandish behaviour such as you'd see in the movies. That was not their son. They didn't want people to think John was like that.

When they read up on the disease, they learned that schizophrenia was a neurological brain disorder on a par with epilepsy or Alzheimer's. Its common symptoms included paranoia, delusional thinking, visual or auditory hallucinations (seeing visions, hearing voices), and deficits in memory, concentration, and motivation. Breakthrough research in the 1980s, using new PET scans, revealed that the structures and blood flow in the brains of people with schizophrenia were markedly different from those in the brains of people without the disease.

Al and Kathleen joined a family education and support group at the Clarke Institute of Psychiatry. Along with some other parents, they founded the Scarborough chapter of the SSO in 1985.

Despite his parents' support and advocacy, John was not getting any better. He went on and off his medications, which was not uncommon for people with mental illness who had difficulty accepting their diagnosis or experienced uncomfortable side effects from the antipsychotics.

The young Birney gradually lost almost everything essential to him: his job, girlfriend, and most of his friends. He lost the ability to look after himself, and his parents advocated for him to live in a supportive housing apartment.

Things became worse in early 1997 when John made two suicide attempts. On the second one, he threw himself off an overpass onto Highway 401. He survived the fall but "broke his back," says Kathleen, and suffered head injuries from which he never fully recovered.

"It's just by the grace of God and his miraculous surgeon that John could still walk," Al often said.

"I don't remember what hospital John was in," Kathleen says. "He was there for a good while, and we went to see him every day, brought him food

CHOOSING THE RIGHT WORDING

One of the guidelines for media reporting on suicides is to avoid saying a person "chose" to end their life.

"You wouldn't say that someone chose to die of cancer or another disease," says Michael McCamus. "Of course, there's an element of choice in people's actions, but for a person killing themself, the person is often robbed of normal, healthy brain functions such as impulse control, deliberation, weighing options, reflection, second thoughts."

Karen Letofsky, the executive director of the Distress Centres of Greater Toronto, says that a suicidal person is acting out of desperation, not choice. "The suicidal person is walking down a long dark hallway. There's a door at the end marked suicide. There are many other doors along the hallway. But the suicidal person does not see them, only the one marked suicide."

The International Risk Management Institute (IRMI), which was founded in 1978 "primarily to educate risk managers, insurance agents/brokers, underwriters, and other insurance professionals," says the concept of choice is confusing.

"While we never have direct access to the inner workings of the mind of someone who has died by suicide, there is much evidence that the thought processes are often gravely disordered by the effects of trauma, mental health conditions, and substance abuse," it says in a 2021 report, "Why Language Matters." "If a person can't choose rationally due to impairment of the mind, the decision is not a choice."

IRMI also discourages the use of *completed* or *committed suicide*, preferring *died of suicide*.

The term *committed suicide* is damaging "because for many, if not most, people it evokes associations with 'committed a crime' or 'committed a sin' and makes us think about something morally reprehensible or illegal," Jacek Debiec, an assistant professor in the University of Michigan's Department of Psychiatry, told HuffPost in March 2019.

In fact, attempting suicide was a criminal offence in Canada until 1972.

> *Committed suicide* also ignores the fact that suicide is often the conse-
> quence of an unaddressed illness, like depression, trauma, or another mental
> health issue, Dan Reidenberg, the executive director of Suicide Awareness
> Voices of Education, told HuffPost. "It should be regarded in the same way as
> any physical health condition."

and stuff. But he was acting up so stupidly, really bad. We hadn't a clue what
was the matter with him."

John was moved to Whitby Mental Health Centre, a large psychiatric hospital in Whitby, the small municipality just east of Toronto. For years, he was
kept in a locked ward, not allowed to leave the hospital. When he had earned
the privilege of going off the grounds with his parents, who regularly visited, he
often asked to go for dinner at Swiss Chalet, one of his favourite places to eat.

"He had clear blue eyes like my father," says Mitch, "and even though
my brother was sick, and he didn't make a lot of sense at times, when he was
lucid, I tell you, there wasn't a nicer guy."

After the initial shock of his son's suicide attempts, Al decided to find
out how many people jumped from bridges in Toronto. He knew from years
of experience that almost every family at the SSO had personal stories of
suicide. He learned that about 40 percent of people with schizophrenia make
an attempt on their lives, and that about 5 to 13 percent die by suicide.

Following weeks of research, Birney realized that the Bloor Street
Viaduct was a suicide magnet on a scale with the Golden Gate Bridge, the
Empire State Building, the Eiffel Tower, Japan's Mount Mihara, and the
Sydney Harbour Bridge in Australia, all of which, except for San Francisco's
iconic suspension bridge, had a barrier of sorts to prevent people from jumping to their deaths. Convincing city hall to erect a barrier and install crisis
phones at Toronto's magnet almost immediately became an obsession.

It was that preoccupation that led Birney to pump up his publicity efforts for Wilson's speech a few months after John's second suicide attempt.
Birney worked hard to get a record turnout for Wilson's appearance, which
he accomplished.

Birney knew he would need help to achieve his goal, given the scale and gravity of the task, but until the night of Michael Wilson's speech, he didn't know where it would come from — until the audience milled about drinking coffee and eating muffins after the speeches had ended. Birney first tried to enlist Michael's younger brother, Peter, to help him, but he declined, suggesting Birney recruit Michael instead.

"Al shook my hand and smiled from ear to ear," says Michael. "He gave me his business card and asked why I was interested in the Schizophrenia Society. I talked about my father. He said, 'Well, why don't you come and help us help the families like yours? That's what we need. We need young, educated people like you.'"

Fascinated by Birney's command of the audience and inspired by the importance of the campaign the older gentleman was determined to pursue, McCamus agreed to join Birney's crusade.

Over the next several years, Birney and McCamus would become close friends and the leading spokespersons of a suicide prevention campaign for the Bloor Viaduct. "It was an evening that changed my life," McCamus says, "and Al's as well."

A few days later, Birney asked the Schizophrenia Society of Ontario, at its annual meeting, to establish "the SSO Bridge Committee" and empower it with "a mandate to campaign for an anti-suicide fence on Toronto's Bloor Street Viaduct" and "any other bridge with a history of suicides or a bridge near a psychiatric facility."

McCamus was late for the June meeting. "By the time I got there, Al had already made the presentation and secured their approval," he says. "He told me that he'd been on the phone for weeks, calling all the chapter presidents and winning their support. He said, 'Never put a motion on the floor unless you know you've got the votes.'"

The SSO voted to make Birney the chair of the Bridge Committee and set aside a few hundred dollars in its budget to cover out-of-pocket expenses such as gas, parking, photocopies, envelopes, postage, and long-distance phone calls.

In September 1997, Birney was also elected president of the East York chapter of the Schizophrenia Society of Ontario.

POSTSCRIPTS

Walter McCamus faithfully took his medications and lived a productive, full life until his death from natural causes in December 2013 at age eighty-one, almost thirty-two years to the day after the worst night of his life, when he had endangered his family's lives in his 1981 near-lethal suicide attempt. His wife, Ruth, who had predeceased him in 2001, called him "a gentle soul." They were married for thirty-three years.

John Birney lived until New Year's Day 2020, spending his last five years at Wyatt Residence, a rural dwelling east of Toronto that provides "a safe and welcoming family-style care facility … to enable mentally ill adults to live assisted in the community," according to its website.

Following his passing, the Wyatt family, which operated the facility, wrote that Johnny-B-Good, as they called him, had a "quick wit and wonderful sense of humour. He loved to read his Bible, sing hymns and he loved to eat!"

Michael Wilson passed away at age eighty-two, in 2019. Although the numerous tributes that emerged following his death celebrated his long political career, they also commended the extensive work he did on behalf of mental health causes. That included having taken on the role of chair of a $10 million fundraising campaign for a new home for the Centre for Addiction and Mental Health (CAMH).

"He [was] as unlikely a hero as one could ever imagine for the mental health movement: A button-down investment banker and no-nonsense Conservative politician known much more for a steely gaze on the bottomline than a bleeding heart," the *Globe*'s André Picard wrote.

Many lauded Wilson's courage in talking openly about his son's illness. But he scoffed at their plaudits. "I reject that," he said. Speaking out was not courageous, but an obligation — to his son, his family, and his community. "How could I do otherwise?" Wilson asked.

"In the early days, we had a running gag about that," says McCamus. "Whenever he'd call me on the phone, I'd answer, 'Yes, my president.' And he'd laugh. Then he'd say, 'I know you're joking, Michael — you can call me Al.'"

In January 1998, the "Bridge Fund" would be increased to two thousand dollars, thanks to contributions from several generous chapters.

"Yes, that's right," says McCamus. "We were supposed to go fight city hall with a committee of two people and two thousand bucks!"

That was the humble beginning of the suicide-barrier campaign for the Bloor Viaduct.

4

The Fatal Attraction of Suicide Magnets

Just before dawn on Sunday, July 12, 1992, thirty-two-year-old Pearl Ann Stewart bundled into her maroon Dodge Shadow, left her home in Mississauga, Ontario, and drove east toward the Bloor Viaduct. She arrived about 5:00 a.m. and briefly lingered near the section of the bridge that leads onto the access ramp for the Don Valley Parkway. Constable Charles Stern, responding to a call from a citizen who saw the woman sitting on the railing overlooking the expressway, carefully guided his police cruiser toward her. He had no idea Stewart's two-and-a-half-year-old son, Robert, was inside the duffel bag she clutched to her chest.

As Stern approached her, Stewart threw the bag over the guardrail and then leapt over after it. Mother and child both died immediately. "Their bodies lay twisted, side by side," the *Toronto Star* reported. "On the floor in the car's back seat area lay a teddy bear, a red balloon, and a child's storybook."

Stewart, originally from Uganda, had been involved in separation and divorce proceedings, the police said.

En route to the viaduct, Stewart likely crossed several bridges from which she could have fulfilled the murder-suicide she felt compelled to play out. But she had selected the viaduct, as had so many distressed souls before her.

In a twist of fate that influenced Michael McCamus's future, his mother, Ruth, a long-time nurse at the Hospital for Sick Children, became a participant in the tragic story.

"That day, two police officers came to her office and asked her to clean up the body of the boy because the child's grandfather was waiting to see the corpse," McCamus says. "She was told: 'Make the body more presentable. Wipe the blood off his face. Clean him up a bit.' As a nurse, my mother had seen children dying. She had seen a lot of devastation, but that really struck her. She came home from work crying that night. She thought that if someone had talked to the woman, maybe that mother and child would still be alive. I always remembered that night, and her reaction, in the years Al and I spent fighting for the barrier." At the time, he adds, there were no crisis telephones at either end of the bridge, a service McCamus would soon lobby for, along with the barrier.

Stewart was by no means the only person to select the Bloor Viaduct as the site to carry out their own death. On May 12, 1997, the Monday after Mother's Day, thirty-six-year-old Ray Doucette Jr. told his mother, Mary, that he loved her, adding, "I'm just going to go for a long drive." That announcement wasn't surprising because his parents had recently bought him a new car to try to cheer him up. Ray had been struggling with mental health issues for years. "He was depressed, and he was paranoid," Ray Doucette Sr. later said.

Ray Jr. left his family's home in Scarborough and drove southwest to the viaduct, parked his new vehicle, and jumped down onto the Don Valley Parkway below. On the way to the viaduct, he passed several other bridges that could have served his desperate plan, as had Stewart. When his father came to collect his dead son's car from the top of the viaduct, he found a can of Coke and a half-eaten sandwich inside.

Ray Jr.'s death wasn't reported, which wasn't unusual. What was out of the ordinary was what his parents did after their son ended his life: They joined the suicide-barrier campaign, one of the few grieving family members to do so.

At Al Birney's urging, the devastated couple had attended the Schizophrenia Society of Ontario (SSO) meeting with Michael Wilson to learn more about the relationship between suicide and mental illness and to be with families confronting this double stigma of a misunderstood disease. It was the beginning of their commitment to support the work Birney, McCamus, and the others were engaged in.

It was likely too painful for other families to keep reminding themselves of what had happened, so almost none chose to go public with their grief.

Later that year, the Doucettes were the first bereaved family who had lost a child at the viaduct that Al Birney met. Their experience had a profound effect on him; perhaps it contributed to a request Birney made to Janice Wiggins, executive director of the SSO: Could he and McCamus sit in on a training session for SSO volunteers that summer, so they could become better educated on the topic of suicide?

Wiggins agreed to have the two men attend a private education and training session for volunteers who dealt with people struggling with suicidal thoughts. She said the volunteers had been experiencing an increasing number of calls from people in crisis, sometimes severe, and many did not feel adequately equipped to handle the weight of the conversations.

The session was led by Karen Letofsky, a suicide expert with two decades of experience at that time. As the executive director of the Distress Centres of Greater Toronto, a non-profit 24-hour crisis hotline staffed by volunteers who answered thousands of calls every month, Letofsky had also pioneered the Survivor Support Program, a support group for families that had experienced suicide.

Letofsky spent several hours listening to the volunteers' concerns and teaching them techniques for handling, and coping with, these challenging calls.

The Three Hs

"Why do people commit suicide?" one volunteer asked at the training session.

"That's a very complicated question," Letofsky said. "Of course, it depends on the individual. But what we talk about at our centre are the three Hs: hopeless, hapless, and helpless."

She explained that many people in crisis feel hopeless that their future will not be better than their present and, therefore, they have no reason to continue living. Hapless is the sense there is a constant dark cloud over your head, and no matter what you do or try, "the rain of trouble" follows you everywhere. When people feel helpless, she said, they believe no one is willing to or capable of helping them. Or, if they suffer from paranoia brought on by mental illness, they don't trust anyone to help them.

Then Birney and McCamus heard a volunteer ask the question they needed answered more than any other, if their suicide-barrier campaign was to succeed: Won't a suicidal person just try another location if the one they first choose isn't available to them? That assumption was logical but not accurate, as Birney and McCamus were about to discover.

Letofsky began her response by talking about ambivalent feelings in some suicidal individuals. She mentioned that some patients of Dr. Jack Kevorkian, the infamous American right-to-die proponent, who had deliberately made plans, over weeks and months, to end their lives through assisted suicide, had changed their minds at the last minute. Those ambivalent feelings, she said, can be an opportunity to help lead the person to help and support, rather than death, as the solution to their suffering.

An article in the *New Yorker* a few years later offered powerful evidence to support Letofsky's contention that some people realize death isn't the right solution for their pain. The author of "Jumpers," Tad Friend, cited two men who had hurled themselves off the Golden Gate Bridge and, against great odds, survived (of the many people who have leapt to their deaths since the bridge was erected, only twenty-five are known to have lived, according to Robert Olson of the Centre for Suicide Prevention, in Calgary, as referenced in a May 2021 article on psycom.net).

"Survivors often regret their decision in midair, if not before," Friend wrote. "Ken Baldwin was twenty-eight and severely depressed on the August day in 1985 when he told his wife not to expect him home till late. 'I wanted to disappear,' he said. 'So the Golden Gate was *the* spot. I'd heard that the water just sweeps you under.' On the bridge, Baldwin counted to ten and stayed frozen. He counted to ten again, then vaulted over. 'I still see my hands coming off the railing [and] instantly realized that everything in my life that I'd thought was unfixable was totally fixable — except for having just jumped.'

"Kevin Hines was eighteen when he took a municipal bus to the bridge one day in September 2000," Friend next wrote. "After treating himself to

FILMING THE BRIDGE

In 2004, Eric Steel and a crew, inspired by Tad Friend's *New Yorker* article, spent a year filming the Golden Gate Bridge during daylight hours. They captured on camera most of the two dozen suicides that occurred that year.

When Steel's documentary, *The Bridge*, was released in 2006, the *New York Times* said it "juxtaposes breathtaking scenes of the Golden Gate and its environs, shot in digital video, with the harrowing personal stories of family members and friends of those who jumped. Because their testimony is remarkably free of religious cant and of cozy New Age bromides, this is one of the most moving and brutally honest films about suicide ever made."

One of the participants was Kevin Hines, who said that four seconds was all it took to plummet the seventy-three metres to the water, which he entered at a speed of approximately 120 kilometres an hour. After surfacing, miraculously still alive, he felt a sea lion nudging his body, helping to keep him afloat until he was rescued by the Coast Guard. He said it was a profound, life-changing experience.

Hines suffered severe damage to his spinal vertebrae and broke his ankle. After he recovered he became a public figure, travelling the world to talk about suicide prevention. Hines detailed his story in a 2018 documentary he produced: *Suicide: The Ripple Effect*. He also authored a memoir, *Cracked Not Broken, Surviving and Thriving After a Suicide Attempt*.

a last meal of Starbursts and Skittles, he paced back and forth and sobbed on the bridge walkway for half an hour. No one asked him what was wrong." One woman, a German tourist, asked him to take her picture. "So I jumped. [But] my first thought was, 'What the hell did I just do? I don't want to die.'"

Letofsky then introduced another factor that could dissuade a person from making a fatal and final decision: if they encounter what experts call *means restriction*. If a person is deprived of their preferred method of taking their life, they don't necessarily substitute another, at least not quickly, she

THE MEANS CAN TRUMP THE ENDS

In a 2022 interview, Karen Letofsky, the former executive director of the Distress Centres of Greater Toronto, offered two examples of *means restriction*. "The first involved [toxic coal] gas stoves in England," she says, referring to a life-saving change in the way the appliance was fuelled.

It was a noteworthy development that Malcolm Gladwell, the best-selling English-born Canadian journalist, wrote about in his book, *Talking to Strangers: What We Should Know About the People We Don't Know*. "In my writing I keep coming back to how important context is in understanding behaviour," he told a *Maclean's* interviewer in 2019.

"I am baffled as to why this is hard for people to understand in regards to suicide," Gladwell continues. "The incidence of suicide is a product of intention in combination with a context. In 1962 when [poet] Sylvia Plath killed herself, like 44 per cent of the other suicides in England and Wales that year, she used the lethal gas in her oven. By the time that gas was fully changed over [from carbon monoxide] to natural gas in 1977, the number of suicides — not just suicide by gas — had plummeted."

Letofsky also cites the seven Chicago-area deaths in 1982 caused by Tylenol capsules laced with potassium cyanide by an unknown person. The manufacturer of the medicine, Johnson & Johnson, took immediate action and introduced tamper-proof packaging, an innovation adapted by the rest of the industry. After doing so no more deaths from this type of sabotage occurred. "The means had been taken away," she says.

said. "We know that some people have a very *specific* plan or vision of how they're going to die. If you can thwart that, they don't automatically go to another place or use another means."

At that point, Birney jumped up, realizing the significance of what she had just said. "You mean, if people are stopped at one bridge, they won't then go to another bridge?" he asked.

"Some people, not all, if they're very fixated on that one location or if they're jumping impulsively," she said. "Yes, you can save some lives."

Birney then excitedly explained that he and McCamus had started a petition to get a barrier on the Bloor Viaduct, which he thrust toward her. "I think there'd be a lot of support for that in the suicide prevention community," she said, as she signed the document.

Although Letofsky's session had provided Birney and McCamus with a critical piece of information, they knew they'd need more evidence if they were to convince city hall that a barrier on the viaduct would prevent some deaths.

The Number One Magnet

The task of assembling proof that suicide magnets existed fell upon Michael McCamus, a relentless and meticulous researcher.

A study of magnets, McCamus knew, had to start with one of the most beautiful structures in the world and, without question, the deadliest — California's Golden Gate Bridge.

Construction of the iconic suspension bridge began in 1933, in the midst of the Great Depression, a time when men were more than willing to brave treacherous working conditions if it meant steady employment. The bridge was no make-work project, however. It would be a much-needed shortcut linking the city of San Francisco with Marin County, as well as the other counties in northern California.

Some 2.73 kilometres long (1.7 miles) and 27.4 metres wide (ninety feet), the Golden Gate was the longest suspension bridge in the world at the time. Two main steel cables containing 128,750 kilometres (eighty thousand miles) of wire passed over the towers. About sixty-seven metres below the roadway, the water sped along the Golden Gate, a strait connecting San Francisco Bay with the Pacific Ocean.

Ten primary contractors took on the task of designing and building the challenging structure; there's no record of how many workers were engaged in the project.

THE STORY OF RUTH

Ruth McCamus was a celebrated pediatric nurse and public education leader at the Hospital for Sick Children in Toronto from 1959 to her retirement in 1995. Well known as a credible source by local journalists, she appeared in media stories every few years.

She was the coordinator of the Family Information Centre, which started in 1979. As the centre's only staff member, Ruth was a fount of information on many topics that parents wanted information about: potty training, sucking thumbs, how to get infants to sleep through the night, facial acne, unsafe toys, the terrible twos, and many others.

In September 1993, she received the inaugural Claus Wirsig Humanitarian Award at SickKids, as the hospital is known colloquially. She is the first and only nurse to receive the coveted award.

Ruth McCamus died of cancer in 2001.

After her death the Alumnae Association of the School of Nursing at the Hospital for Sick Children solicited donations for the newly created "Ruth Duncan McCamus Award for Family-Centred Nursing," a bursary for pediatric nurses. From 2002 to 2011, ten recipients were each awarded a two-thousand-dollar scholarship for graduate studies in nursing in Ruth's name.

What is known is that none of them fell to their deaths, despite the high winds and often precarious footing. That's because chief engineer Joseph Baermann Strauss insisted a net be installed under the bridge, at a cost of $130,000, to catch any falling workers; it was believed his concern was, first and foremost, for their safety (he also enforced the wearing of hard hats, made out of leather). He also perceived that every death would delay construction, which he was steadfastly determined would finish on time, if not beforehand (he accomplished the latter goal). Nineteen men did indeed plunge into the net; all survived.

The bridge was completed in 1937 and was hailed as an engineering and artistic marvel. It offered spectacular views, including that of Alcatraz Island, the home of the infamous penitentiary, as well as Angel Island, known as "Ellis Island West," where immigrants from East Asia entered America.

On May 27, a day before the bridge officially welcomed both vehicle and pedestrian traffic, a week-long Golden Gate Fiesta began. There were fireworks, a performance by *The Jazz Singer* star Al Jolson, and a visit from Canada's red-coated Royal Canadian Mounted Police. The next morning, President Franklin Delano Roosevelt pressed a telegraph key in Washington, signalling the bridge's official christening.

One of the most striking aspects of the bridge was its "golden" colour. In a 2022 interview with the *Nob Hill Gazette*, Denis Mulligan, the general manager and CEO of the bridge, explained how it came to be.

"The Navy thought there should be yellow and black diagonal stripes on the towers, like an old barbershop pole, so it would stand out," he said. "They were scared the bridge was so big, planes were going to fly into it. People thought it should be gray, like the San Francisco-Oakland Bay Bridge. Some said green. And the arguments ensued. Eventually, they started building the bridge and they brought out the steel from Pennsylvania, and it had a red lead primer on it, which was a burnt orange color. People looked at the color of the primer and said, 'Wow, that's it.'"

Sadly, this magnificent engineering and artistic accomplishment — one of the world's largest examples of the art-deco style — soon developed a sinister side akin to the Bloor Viaduct. Its beauty, grandeur, and renown turned it almost immediately into a suicide magnet.

The first known jumper was forty-seven-year-old Harold Wobber of Oakland, California, a First World War veteran who had resided for many years in a hospital for the insane. He reportedly turned to a stranger on the bridge and handed him his jacket. "This is as far as I go," he said, and jumped over the rail. His body was never found.

Wobber effortlessly killed himself because the safety net had been taken down once construction ended, for aesthetic reasons. Chief engineer Strauss, who died of a heart attack in 1938 at age fifty-eight, likely influenced its removal when he said, in 1936, that "the Golden Gate Bridge is practically suicide proof. Suicide from the bridge is neither possible nor probable."

Buoyed by that unfortunate declaration, local authorities issued another, equally foolhardy, directive. The original design for the bridge called for a higher railing specifically to protect against suicides. In a last-minute decision, this safety feature was sacrificed for the view.

With the safety features removed, approximately two thousand people have jumped off the Golden Gate Bridge, at the time of this writing. The total is likely much higher because an unknown number of bodies have been washed out to sea. "Other times the body is found, but far enough away that the death cannot be attributed with certainty to the bridge," John Bateson wrote in his 2012 book, *The Final Leap: Suicide on the Golden Gate Bridge*.

In a troubling footnote, Golden Gate Bridge suicides have long intrigued the media and the public, sometimes to a disturbing degree, journalist Ann Garrison wrote in a 1998 essay, "Our Beautiful, Lethal Bridge." "San Francisco had been accused of taking a perverse pride in its reputation. Tour bus drivers cited the death toll as they passed the bridge; the city's daily papers announced each leap."

The *New Yorker*'s Tad Friend noted that "in the eighties, workers at a local lumberyard formed 'the Golden Gate Leapers Association' — a sports pool in which bets were placed on which day of the week someone would jump."

This morbid fascination with the jumpers was stoked by some media outlets, Friend wrote. "The coverage intensified in 1973, when the *Chronicle* and the *Examiner* initiated countdowns to the five-hundredth recorded jumper. Bridge officials turned back fourteen aspirants to the title, including one man who had '500' chalked on a cardboard sign pinned to his T-shirt. The eventual 'winner,' who eluded both bridge personnel and local television crews, was a commune dweller tripping on LSD.

In 1995, as number 1,000 approached, the frenzy was even greater. A local disk jockey went so far as to promise a case of Snapple to the family of the victim. That June, trying to stop the countdown fever, the California Highway Patrol halted its official count at 997. In early July, Eric Atkinson,

HOW IRONIC

"Jim Jones, leader of the Peoples Temple, delivered one of the most momentous bridge soliloquies, on Memorial Day 1977, when he and a group of his followers joined 400 anti-suicide activists in the bridge toll plaza to commemorate bridge suicides and demand the erection of a preventive barrier atop the railing," Ann Garrison wrote in her 1998 essay, "Our Beautiful, Lethal Bridge."

"Jones, by then feeling persecuted by defectors, media and government, told the crowd that he had been in a suicidal mood himself that day, and that he had personal empathy for what we are doing here today. The next year, on November 18, 1978, he died of suicide and 913 followers died in what was considered a mass murder at their compound in Guyana."

age twenty-five, became the unofficial thousandth; he was seen jumping, but his body was never found.

"Ken Holmes, the Marin County coroner, told [Friend], 'When the number got to around eight hundred and fifty, we went to the local papers and said, "You've *got* to stop reporting numbers."'"

Perhaps as a result of such egregious behaviour, the Centers for Disease Control and Prevention and the American Association of Suicidology issued guidelines urging the media to downplay the suicides. Jumps are rarely reported anymore unless they involve a celebrity or severely snarl traffic. "We weaned them," Holmes said, "[but] the lack of publicity hasn't reduced the number of suicides at all."

The Tale of Two Bridges

As McCamus delved into the available information about suicide magnets, he learned that the San Francisco-Oakland Bay Bridge, known by locals as the Bay Bridge, experienced far fewer suicides than the Golden Gate Bridge.

Located less than six miles apart, both bridges had been completed by 1937 and were about the same height. The gray-coloured Bay Bridge, however, had none of the romantic allure of its sister bridge, which awed visitors with its striking beauty. Likely as a result, it was not a suicide magnet.

A 1982 study of the two bridges, by Richard Seiden and Mary Spence of the University of California, Berkeley, noted that "there are substantially more suicides from the Golden Gate Bridge." This was based on their analysis of data from 1937 through 1979. They concluded, in somewhat academic

A COMPELLING STUDY

In 1978, Dr. Richard Seiden published a seminal work: "Where Are They Now? A Follow-Up Study of Suicide Attempters from the Golden Gate Bridge."

"From the opening day, May 18, 1937 to April 1, 1978, there have been 625 officially reported suicide deaths and perhaps more than 200 others which have gone unseen and unreported," the abstract to his paper began.

"Proposals for the construction of a hardware anti-suicide barrier have been challenged with the untested contention that 'they'll just go some-place else.' This research tests the contention by describing and evaluating the long-term mortality experience of the 515 persons who had attempted suicide from the Golden Gate Bridge but were restrained, from the opening day through the year 1971 plus a comparison group of 184 persons who made nonbridge suicide attempts during 1956–57 and were treated at the emergency room of a large metropolitan hospital and were also followed through the close of 1971.

"Results of the follow-up study are directed toward answering the important question: 'Will a person who is prevented from suicide in one location inexorably tend to attempt and commit suicide elsewhere?'

"What this [study] discloses is that after 26-plus years the vast majority of GGB [Golden Gate Bridge] suicide attempters (about 94%) are still alive or have died from natural causes."

wording, that "suggestion plays some part in the differential suicide experience and that psychological/symbolic factors play an even more significant part in the choice of the Golden Gate Bridge and its reputation as a suicide landmark."

On a more anecdotal note, Eve Meyer, executive director of San Francisco Suicide Prevention, told a San Francisco media website in 2006 that "while officials carefully count jumpers from the Golden Gate, it's difficult to find anyone who similarly tracks Bay Bridge suicides." She estimated that "three or four people leap to their deaths from the Bay Bridge each year, compared with an average of 19 a year on the Golden Gate."

McCamus then came upon another landmark study that also compared two neighbouring bridges, both located in Washington, D.C., and the decision to erect a barrier on only one of them.

Presented at the 1993 annual meeting of the American Association of Suicidology by two MDs, Patrick O'Carroll and Morton Silverman, a paper entitled "Community Suicide Prevention: The Effectiveness of Bridge Barriers" compared suicide rates at the Duke Ellington Bridge and the William Howard Taft Bridge.

The former honoured Edward Kennedy "Duke" Ellington, the celebrated twentieth-century pianist, composer, and leader of his eponymous orchestra; the bridge was named after him in 1974. The latter was named for America's twenty-seventh president.

William Howard Taft was an accomplished politician but lacked the charisma of his predecessor, Teddy Roosevelt. He also struggled with his weight, ballooning to almost 160 kilograms (350 pounds) by the end of his term. When later serving as chief justice of the United States, he began walking to shed some of his bulk. His daily routine took him over a bridge spanning Rock Creek Park. A year after his death in 1930, it was named the Taft Bridge.

The bridges, which are located not far from each other, both span Rock Creek. They're about the same height and both stand about forty metres (131 feet) above a roadway. The authors found that "from 1979 through 1985, there were 24 suicides from [the Duke Ellington], double the number (12) from the neighbouring Taft Bridge." Interestingly, the total suicides from the two structures "equaled 50% of all leaps recorded from all the approximately 330 bridges in D.C. during those years."

In 1985, following three suicides in a ten-day period, "and as a result of lobbying efforts by Ben Read, a former Deputy Secretary of State whose 24-year-old daughter had previously jumped to her death from [the Ellington], the mayor [Marion Barry] ordered the construction of an 8-foot-high anti-suicide fence [on the Ellington]," the authors wrote. It cost approximately $230,000. Almost from the outset, "the project was opposed by the National Trust for Historic Preservation and by seven neighborhood groups (including the Art Deco Society)."

The authors reported that the opposition centred on three primary contentions: a fence blocked scenic views, the architectural integrity of the bridge would be compromised, and "fences do not prevent suicides; substitutes would be found." Because of the unsuccessful but vociferous campaign to stop the barrier at the Duke Ellington, a plan to erect one at the Taft was scuttled.

THE TAFT NEEDS A BARRIER

Following the death by suicide of twenty-nine-year-old Dr. Peter Tripp on April 13, 2022, at the Taft Bridge, his partner, Dr. Chelsea Van Thof, began a campaign to convince the city to install suicide barriers on the bridge.

"Tripp had no documented history of mental illness, did not voice concerns or struggles to his partner and had never sought mental health support," the *Wash* reported. "If a barrier had been on the bridge, Van Thof said she believes Tripp could have received help.

"Successful suicides are impulse decisions, and that's why this barrier is so important," Van Thof said. "I know that if it was there, it would have cut through that impulse for Peter."

After recent media coverage on the barrier movement, Van Thof said she is optimistic and "definitely seeing progress."

O'Carroll and Silverman were not swayed by the opponents. They reported that the number of suicides on the Taft did not significantly increase after the barrier was erected on the Ellington. If it was true that jumpers would just look for another bridge, O'Carroll and Silverman argued that, logically, the number of deaths from the adjacent Taft should have markedly increased. "I would strongly recommend that the barriers remain intact and that other preventive interventions be explored and implemented for the other popular jump sites in the city [such as the Taft Bridge]," Silverman concluded.

The study and its enthusiastic endorsement of barriers on suicide magnets added to the evidence McCamus was amassing for the presentations he and Birney were planning to make to Toronto City Council.

"When Al and I were doing research in 1997, it wasn't easy," he says. "The internet was embryonic. We couldn't find studies on the web. In those days, the way to get copies of academic papers took a lot of time and effort. You had to go to libraries and spend hours ferreting them out.

MUCH-NEEDED HELP

In October 1997, Birney and McCamus read in a mental health newsletter that the University of Toronto had created the Arthur Sommer Rotenberg Chair in Suicide and Depression Studies in the memory of Arthur, a thirty-six-year-old doctor who had killed himself in November 1992.

To honour his memory, his mother, Doris, endowed the chair for the study of suicide. In January 1997, Dr. Paul Links, a psychiatry professor at the University of Toronto and a psychiatrist at Wellesley Central Hospital, became the first chair. Its ultimate purpose was "to reduce the losses and suffering from suicide and suicidal behaviours." The program was, at the time, the only one of its kind in North America.

"It became an invaluable resource," says McCamus, "and Dr. Links became an important member of our volunteer group."

"I felt confident we had enough information from these two studies, and from others I found, to convince the politicians to support our campaign," McCamus says. He is also a pragmatist, however, and a famous quote elbowed its way into his brain. It was attributed to former U.S. member of congress Earl Landgrebe, who supported President Richard Nixon during the Watergate investigations: "Don't confuse me with the facts. I've got a closed mind."

McCamus hoped history wouldn't repeat itself, but he had his doubts. He was determined, though, to find out. He and Birney got together and decided to begin lobbying the councillors individually — all fifty-six of them.

5

Ken Dryden Reacts Personally

Growing up in the former city of Etobicoke, Ken Dryden, who was born in 1947, had little, if any, knowledge of the Bloor Viaduct, and certainly didn't know anything about its dark history. In those days, many families living in the western outskirts of Toronto rarely ventured east of the big city's downtown core.

Five months after he was appointed president of the Toronto Maple Leafs in May 1997, the NHL Hall of Fame goalie and accomplished author would learn it was the location where Martin Kruze took his life, after enduring years of pain from the sexual abuse he'd been subjected to at Maple Leaf Gardens.

When Dryden had assumed the presidency, he'd been briefed on many matters, including the sex scandal, although he has only a faint memory of what he'd been told. "I was aware the Leafs' lawyers were working on it, but beyond that I don't really recall," he says.

He had, like most people, heard stories of abuse happening in religious and educational institutions and had not liked the way in which many of the culpable bodies had responded to the allegations after the fact. "I could understand what was being said but it wasn't satisfactory," he says. "Here was this very human, personal story, and the responses were all impersonal. They were almost always by lawyers, occasionally by spokespeople, and [their] tone [was] not right."

In August 1997, Dryden received a letter from Martin Kruze. "He said he wanted to do something for child-abuse survivors, and not just for those from the Gardens, and was asking for our help. I put the letter into a small 'get to' pile on my desk," Dryden wrote some fifteen years later. "Then the Leafs' training camp opened, then the season began — and then I got a call. It was from a policeman. Martin Kruze had jumped off [the viaduct] and died."

Did Dryden ever wonder what might have happened if he'd responded to the letter?

"I don't know," he says, in his halting way of speaking. "I mean, you know … it could have been. And, you know, I … I was slow on the pickup, I mean, I … I should have responded sooner."

After Martin Kruze jumped to his death in October 1997, Dryden decided he would try to do the right thing, not react impersonally as he had observed others doing in the past. "I remember a day or so afterward thinking, I need to go to the funeral," he says.

He wasn't sure if he'd be welcome. "I knew I had to contact the Kruze family, to ask them if I had the right to go to the funeral," he says.

Dryden telephoned the home of Martin's mother, Astrida, where Martin's brother Gary, and Gary's wife, Teresa, had gathered. Dryden was unaware that Teresa was the TSN sports broadcaster he had seen on TV. Once that connection had been made, Teresa urged him to attend, saying, "'the family would want you there,'" he says. "She was terrific."

Gary remembers saying, "Absolutely, absolutely. We'd be honoured to have you there."

In mid-November, Dryden paid his respects at a public memorial for Martin held at St. Andrew's Latvian Lutheran Church in downtown Toronto. "The church was not far from the Gardens," he says. "I just walked [there] by myself."

An Important Insight

As he listened to the eulogies, thinking everyone there "wanted to punch me in the nose as a representative of the Leafs," he came to a powerful insight: "Gradually, it became completely clear that what the family wanted more than anything was that something, a little bit of good, comes out of something so bad. And I was, oh, shoot, that's what I should have understood right from the beginning."

A few days later, Dryden organized a meeting with members of the Kruze family, as well as a few others, to explore what could be done to honour Martin's life. "He said he didn't want to sweep it under the carpet," Gary says. "We met with Ken several times in his office. And then he arranged, maybe a couple months later, for us to meet with twenty agencies across Canada, in particular in Ontario, to see if they would, you know, join and do something about [the abuse problem]."

Dryden also ordered the flags at the Gardens be lowered to half-mast. "That gesture seemed only fitting, given that the flags had been lowered 13 years ago upon the death of George Hannah, the longtime Gardens' equipment manager — and one of those who, it turned out, had abused Kruze," *Maclean's* reported.

One central idea emerged from the meetings Dryden convened. "We needed to have some kind of public way to talk about abuses and sexual abuse," he says. "Something that generated conversation, awareness, and understanding, and knowledge that didn't exist before." The location for these "forums," as they became known, had to be Maple Leaf Gardens, Dryden believed. "It happened in the Gardens; the response should be at the Gardens. I mean, if the lousy thing happened here, the little bit of a good thing should happen here, too. It shouldn't happen in some sort of outside space, different space, somewhere else, some place distant, disconnected. No, it should happen here at the most public, best-known building in Toronto."

On January 23, 1998, Dryden made good on his commitment to do the right thing.

Steve Stavro, chairman and the chief executive of Maple Leaf Gardens, publicly apologized to the ninety-plus young men who had been victimized at the historic arena during the 1970s and early eighties. Dryden stood beside him during the announcement, which the Leafs had been criticized for not making sooner.

"All of us at Maple Leaf Gardens are deeply saddened that children were [sexually] abused in this building," a visibly shaken Stavro told a news conference, the *Toronto Star* reported.

He specifically addressed the family of Martin Kruze, who were present. "I want to see that such things never happen again," he said.

Stavro and Dryden unveiled a program for the victims. "Among the initiatives were a support hotline; an annual [event] at the Gardens on child abuse [called the Martin Arnold Kruze Memorial Forum]; payment for counselling, and placement and training in government-retaining programs, or other life- or work-skills programs; organizing new events and donating the use of the Gardens to help raise money for charities that deal with child abuse," the *Star* article said.

An educational gathering on the topic of child abuse invited students from the Toronto District and Toronto Catholic District School Boards to attend. By 2003, the Leafs reported that "more than 2,000 elementary and secondary students from schools across Toronto have participated" in the initiative.

Stavro also said the Gardens had put in place a program to screen employees for a history of child sexual abuse. "I know that Martin is listening, and this is what he wanted to happen," said Jayne Dunsmore, Kruze's partner.

WELL INTENTIONED, POORLY ATTENDED

Three forums to explore issues involving sexual abuse of children were held, two at Maple Leaf Gardens and one at Toronto's Delta Chelsea Hotel. Michael Burgess sang at the first one, and prominent Maple Leafs, including Ken Dryden, Darryl Sittler, and Wendel Clark, took part.

"The two Maple Leaf Gardens forums were good," says Gary Kruze. "We had something like fifty agencies set up booths. But not as many people attended as we thought would come. Maybe a thousand. The one at the Delta fizzled."

The reason for the low turnout, he came to realize, was that other than survivors and their friends and families, "people didn't want to be there, by association, because people might think, well maybe you were abused."

"I feel sad it took Martin Kruze's death to bring [all] this about," former NHLer Sheldon Kennedy, who was in attendance at the 1998 announcement, said. He had been sexually abused by his coach, Graham James, when he played in the Western Hockey League from the mid to late 1980s. "Death is a reality in this situation. I've been there and thank God someone was there to grab me and drag me the other way."

"I Was the Bait"

In late February 2012, Ken Dryden wrote "a personal essay" in the *Globe and Mail*, triggered by "the stomach-twisting story of the abuse" former NHL star Theo Fleury had suffered at the hands of his junior hockey coach, "the now-infamous Graham James."

At the end of the essay, Dryden shared what he called a final story, about another victim of the Maple Leaf Gardens pedophile ring: "We had met before. Then, some weeks later, we saw each other again at a Leafs press conference, nodded and smiled. This was a year or two after Martin Kruze's death. When the event ended, he came over. 'I used to love you,' he said. 'Then I hated you.' He was about 40, tall, with thinning hair and a mustache. 'I dreamed I was you,' he told me. 'I loved hockey. I was tall. I was a goalie in every game I played. My parents bought me some brand-new equipment. I was you,' he repeated. His 10-year-old self came back to life, in his voice and eyes. 'I used to hang around outside the Gardens. I just wanted to see the players, any of them, live. An older guy who worked there somehow knew I really liked you — maybe I told him. He said he knew you. He said he could introduce me — when you were in town.' His voice and eyes began to change. 'That's how it began. Then I hated you,' he said, his hatred worn by time now gone from his voice. 'One morning, I went downstairs, picked up that new equipment and threw it into a garbage pail. I told my parents it'd been stolen. I never played again.'"

"I was the bait," Dryden realized, connecting him directly to the horror that had left such a terrible stain on one of Canada's most iconic institutions.

MARTIN, SHELDON, AND OPRAH

In 1997, Oprah Winfrey invited Sheldon Kennedy and his wife, Jana, on her TV program to discuss the abuse Sheldon suffered at the hands of his coach, Graham James.

After the interview she brought out Martin Kruze to talk about what he had experienced.

The segment ended with the wives of the Philadelphia Flyers, an NHL team Kennedy had never even played for, presenting him with a cheque for fifty thousand dollars for the charity he had founded along with former player, turned agent, Tom Laidlaw.

The following year, after Kruze had ended his life, Kennedy decided to roller-blade across Canada to raise awareness and funds for sexual abuse victims.

A few days after visiting Prime Minister Jean Chrétien on Canada Day, Kennedy skated west to Toronto. "When we came to the Bloor Street Viaduct, I stopped for a while," he wrote in his 2006 biography, *Why I Didn't Say Anything*.

"As I looked down at the Don Valley far below, I thought about how much Martin would have enjoyed this day. It might have made him feel a little better to see how many people were getting out to support the cause. At the same time, I could understand why he had killed himself that day. I can remember many occasions where I felt so low that the only thing that made me feel better was the thought of suicide, of escaping from my own skin and escaping this world."

Kennedy's cross-country skate raised approximately $3 million.

Justice (Partly) Meted Out

Between 1977 and 2020, Loretta Merritt of Torkin Manes represented thirty survivors of the sexual abuse they endured at Maple Leaf Gardens.

All cases were settled out of court. She says the Maple Leafs were "generally pretty good" in their interactions with her. "They dealt with the

KEN DRYDEN REACTS PERSONALLY

survivors in a respectful manner. They worked with Ellen Campbell from the Canadian Centre for Abuse Awareness to set up a fund for interim therapy for people. They hired a decent and respectful defence council."

She does mention "one crazy story" a client told her. "A couple of very senior people from Maple Leaf Gardens pulled up to my client's donut shop in a limo. I say my client's donut shop because he dealt drugs from a particular shop. He didn't own it. They rolled down the window and offered him cash to settle the case." He declined.

Although questionable, what they did was perfectly legal.

Merritt isn't allowed to say the amount of any of the settlements. But she does suggest reading, on her website, a 2015 article she wrote, "Why Are Damages in Sexual Abuse Cases So Low?" It particularly addresses her contention that there is a "bias against psychological injuries" compared to how the system reacts to physical injuries. "Having spoken to hundreds of survivors over the last twenty years, it is my view that a psychological injury can in fact be more disabling than a physical injury."

THE FATE OF THE PERPS

George Hannah died in 1984, of kidney failure, without ever facing charges for his crimes.

John Paul Roby was convicted in 1999 of thirty counts of assault involving the sexual abuse of young boys at the Gardens. He was declared a dangerous offender in 2000 and died of a heart attack in prison the following year.

Gordon Stuckless pleaded guilty in 1997 to twenty-four counts of sexual and indecent assault. He was sentenced to two years less a day and three years' probation. Judge David Watt, wanting to protect the public from Stuckless in the future, offered the light sentence in return for Stuckless agreeing to take chemical castration medication.

Nonetheless, the sentence was increased to six years on appeal, less a year for time served.

Stuckless was freed on statutory release in 2001 after serving two-thirds of his sentence.

In 2013, he was rearrested and charged with almost one hundred counts of indecent assault on a male, assault, and possession of a weapon or imitation. He pleaded guilty to the charges.

Stuckless wasn't sentenced until June 2016; he received six and a half years behind bars — six after credit for his time on house arrest.

Teresa Kruze noted that Jerry Sandusky, the former U.S. assistant football coach at Penn State, was sentenced to between thirty and sixty years (with no chance of parole until at least thirty years had been served) for abusing fewer victims.

"You ruined generations, you fucking creep," one victim screamed out as Stuckless was escorted out of the courtroom. "You should rot in jail," Gary Kruze shouted at Stuckless outside the courtroom.

A man, who can only be identified as J.D., said the abuse he suffered at age eleven at Maple Leaf Gardens filled him with self-loathing and hopelessness.

"I'm fifty-two years old and I'm still broken inside," he said, adding he kept his "dark secret" under wraps for close to forty years.

Stuckless was released to a halfway house on day parole in December 2019 and died of a brain hemorrhage the following April in a Hamilton hospital. "Martin would be absolutely livid [that he was released]," Teresa told the *Toronto Sun*. "It's appalling."

Less known than the three main perpetrators was former Gardens security guard Dennis Morin. In 2002, he was found guilty of sexual assault, indecent assault, and gross indecency for incidents involving teenage boys and was handed a three-and-a-half-year sentence.

Gary and Teresa Kruze's Crusade

Through their interactions with Ken Dryden, Gary and Teresa met Ellen Campbell, who had founded the Centre for Abuse Awareness (now Abuse

Hurts). A childhood sexual abuse survivor, Campbell in 1993 held the first National Conference for Adult Survivors of Sexual Abuse.

In alliance with Gary and Teresa, Maple Leaf Sports & Entertainment, and Shoppers Drug Mart, the centre founded the Martin Kruze Memorial Fund, which continues in operation today. Abuse Hurts managed the trust accounts for the Gardens' survivors until the trusts ran out and continues to manage the therapy for the men.

It also operates, in addition to other support services, Time for Men, and the Help & Hope Project. Both are peer support programs offered at no cost to the men and facilitated by a qualified therapist.

Gary and Teresa became advocates for hundreds of survivors. They supported legal reform, especially changes to what they believed were inadequate, lenient sentences for sexual predators. They also worked with John Muise, the former head of the sex crimes division for the Toronto Police Service, who had joined the board of the centre as its director of public safety.

In June 2007, Campbell and Muise presented a three hundred–page report, *Martin's Hope*, to a parliamentary committee considering "Bill C-27, An Act to amend the Criminal Code (dangerous offenders and recognizance to keep the peace)." It was Martin's hope, says Gary, that "if he could save even one child from going through what he went through, then you know, his life wouldn't be in vain."

"Prime Minister Stephen Harper adopted the report," says Gary. "He invited us to Ottawa when the bill was being debated. Then we had a nice reception with [him] for a couple of hours. It was wonderful. He was a real support all through this."

The report, which had first been released in late 2004, had sixty recommendations for change — thirty-nine directed at the federal government, and twenty-one at the Ontario provincial government.

What primarily came out of that initiative was the decision by the federal government to raise the age of consent from fourteen to sixteen. "That was huge," Gary says. "Prime Minister Harper got that done."

After Justin Trudeau became prime minister in 2015, Gary and Teresa encountered a different reception from the new Liberal government.

"My husband and I were trying to get the government to change how they deal with pedophiles," Teresa told the *Toronto Sun* in 2019, adding that after a promising start the powerful have turned their backs. "We got nowhere on tougher sentencing. They weren't interested at all in toughening the legal system against sex criminals."

6

The Stars Align

The official campaign to erect a safety barrier and crisis phones on Toronto's most infamous bridge took place in a political landscape rocked by a tectonic change.

On January 1, 1998, a new megacity was created through the amalgamation of Scarborough, Etobicoke, North York, the city of York, the borough of East York, and Toronto. The transformation, which was extremely unpopular in Toronto, was imposed by the provincial Conservative government of Premier Mike Harris. Campaigning on a "Common Sense Revolution" platform, Harris had won a landslide victory in the 1995 election. He cited cost saving as the impetus behind the dramatic change.

"The amalgamation was — and still is — one of the most controversial moves in Toronto's local government history," the *Toronto Star* would express sixteen years later, adding that "76 percent of [downtown] voters were opposed to the merger."

For Birney and McCamus, who were set to launch a lobbying effort to build support for their initiative, it meant dealing with a new chief magistrate — Mel Lastman, longtime mayor of North York and founder of the Bad Boy furniture chain — and many politicians who had no affiliation with downtown Toronto or knowledge of the issues involving the Bloor Viaduct.

Lastman was a particular problem. A charismatic salesman, he had the common touch but lacked the political sophistication of the incumbent, liberal-minded Barbara Hall, who he easily defeated in the election of 1997. "While Hall was cast as the protector of both the centrality of Toronto urbanity and of the metropolis's marginal populations, Lastman became the popular spokesman for the small taxpayers in the inner suburbs, as well as the champion of most business interests," Julie-Anne Boudreau, Roger Keil, and Douglas Young wrote in their 2009 book, *Changing Toronto: Governing Urban Neoliberalism.*

Hall made homelessness one of her main campaign platforms; Lastman, on the other hand, famously declared during the election that North York, where he had been mayor from 1973 to the end of 1997, didn't have any homeless people. That ludicrous claim was exposed for its vacuousness when a homeless woman, forty-eight-year-old Linda Houston, who suffered from paranoid schizophrenia, died in North York a day after he uttered the untrue comment.

Birney and McCamus would discover the extent of Lastman's ignorance in the years ahead when he confessed to being unaware of where the viaduct was located — a stunning admission, like the mayor of New York not knowing the location of the Brooklyn Bridge — and by often referring to it as the Prince Edward Island Viaduct, perhaps thinking it had something to do with Canada's smallest province.

A Little Booklet Helps a Great Deal

In early January 1998, to complement the swearing-in of the new fifty-six-member council, every household in the amalgamated city received in the mail a little blue-and-white booklet that included a phone directory of city services, as well as a phone and fax number for every councillor's office.

"It was invaluable," says McCamus. "I almost immediately started mailing out information packages to the councillors in batches of two, three, or four every few days."

Each package contained two newspaper articles about suicides from the viaduct, a photo of the chain-link fence on the Glen Street Bridge in Glens Falls, New York, a copy of a letter from the New York State Department of

Transportation explaining its rationale for putting fences on some bridges, a brochure from the Schizophrenia Society of Ontario (SSO), and a letter from Birney on SSO letterhead requesting a meeting. The cost of the envelope and postage was more than one dollar per package, a substantial amount that came out of their meagre budget.

"This letter and the attached documentation will demonstrate that: (1) deaths from Toronto's Bloor Street Viaduct are an alarming, yet preventable, public concern; (2) the Schizophrenia Society of Ontario's advocacy of safety measures to deter bridge suicide has precedents in other large municipalities; and (3) Toronto City Council could demonstrate pioneering leadership, and win favour from families of the mentally ill, by taking concerted and public action against bridge suicides," Birney wrote. "The time has come to erect safety fences along the Bloor Street Viaduct, and to install crisis/hot line telephones on each of the bridge's sidewalks."

LOW TECH

An impoverished student at the time, McCamus wrote the letters on a Dell 486 computer running Windows 3.0. "Most of my friends were running Windows 95 or 98 by then," he says. "The computer probably had a 40 MHz processor. It didn't have an internet connection. I printed the letters on a small Canon inkjet printer. The technology was outdated even by 1998 standards."

Pots and Pans Diplomacy

Birney and McCamus wanted to send one of their packages to Mayor Lastman but knew his plate would be full of other priorities more important than the viaduct. They needed a way to jump the queue.

"Al remembered he had a connection with Paul Godfrey, a close friend of Lastman, from decades back," says McCamus, referencing the former Metro Toronto chairperson and, at the time, CEO of Sun Media. "I believe Godfrey was a high school or university student when Al trained him to sell sets of stainless cookware to suburban housewives door-to-door."

Mitch remembers that his father "would go over to people's houses, and he would be a pitch man. And he would sell the pots and pans to all the young girls, a lot of them nurses, that came over from England. They wouldn't be married yet, and of course, they needed a good set of pots and pans or they weren't gonna get a husband, apparently."

Al, never a shrinking violet, phoned Godfrey's office at Sun Media.

When Godfrey called back, McCamus remembers the conversation. "Al said something like, 'You know what I did last night just for fun, Paul? I went down to the basement and got all the old pots and pans. I brought them upstairs and laid them out on the kitchen table, just like the old days. And I did our old presentation for Kathleen and Michael. Right there in the kitchen. Do you remember that?'"

"Yes, of course," said Godfrey, laughing out loud.

"Now, would you like to pay by cash today or four easy installments by cheque? If you pay today, we have this special gift," Birney said, recreating their closing pitch.

Godfrey laughed some more.

"So Paul, you know I'm working on the bridge, the viaduct. My son jumped from a bridge, and we've got to get a letter to Lastman. Can you help us, Paul?"

Godfrey said sure and asked Birney to send him the package. Birney said he would bring it to Godfrey's office "tomorrow morning if you like."

For a while, they didn't know if Lastman ever got the package. Finally, Birney got a phone call saying that the mayor's office was "going to wait to see what comes out of committee." It was a political response that said nothing specific, but it proved that Paul Godfrey had done what he had promised.

To their collective credit, one by one the councillors had an assistant call to book a time for Birney and McCamus to visit them. "Al would pick me up at my house in the new, big, green Bonneville his company, Cook

Al Birney (left) and Michael McCamus in front of Toronto city hall.

Transport, had given him as a retirement gift," McCamus says. "He always kept his parking receipts so he could be reimbursed by the SSO."

As they walked to their appointment, Birney would repeat his sales philosophy: "Michael, you sell yourself. You sell your company. Sell your product. Then get out of there before they change their minds."

Before embarking on the meetings, the two men discussed what they should request from the councillors. "I always watched the evening news," McCamus says. "I had noticed that when families or survivors were asked what response was needed to a tragedy, they often gave vague answers, such as: 'I want justice for my son.' Or, 'My daughter's death should not be in vain.' We decided to ask for something more specific."

They opted for three commitments from each councillor: vote for the installation of a safety fence and emergency phones on the viaduct; sign their SSO petition to show they endorsed the suicide prevention project; and sign a letter of support for the project that they could show other councillors and the media. "We figured if a councillor did all three things, they were a genuine supporter," Birney said.

A Lesson in Politics

The first politician Birney and McCamus met with was Michael Prue, a friendly forty-nine-year-old progressive who had served as the mayor of East York until amalgamation (in 2022, he was elected mayor of Amherstburg, a small town in southwestern Ontario, not far from Detroit). Often smiling, Prue sported a moustache that made him look like the actor Hal Linden, the star of a late seventies TV series, *Barney Miller*. "When I was younger and I knocked on doors, people would scream: 'Come to the door! Barney Miller's here!'" Prue says.

Ever the salesman, Birney opened with some small talk and corny humour, a common icebreaker he employed. "Want to see a picture of my wife? She's my pride and joy," he'd ask, to which the person invariably said yes. Birney would then pull a card out of his wallet that featured two cleaning products: Pride furniture wax and Joy dish soap. Comedian Henny Youngman had created the joke cards in the 1960s. It could have been an embarrassing overture but somehow the likeable Birney pulled it off.

Not long after the two men had started their pitch, Prue told them that when he was in high school in the 1960s, a student he knew jumped to his death from the viaduct.

"You don't have to convince me of your campaign," he said. "I'm going to support it."

But when they asked him to sign their petition and write a letter they could share with other councillors, they received a quick lesson in local politics.

"That's not the way council works," Prue said, in an annoyed tone.

"Why not?" McCamus said.

"Because city councillors do not tell each other how to vote."

Councillors make decisions based on reports, he explained. A city hall committee assigns city bureaucrats to research an issue or problem, talk to some stakeholders, and then issue a report with recommendations. Then the councillors debate it and vote on the report. Everything hinges on the report.

Years later, Prue remembers his first meeting with them. "They were two rookies, I tell you. I was a little skeptical, at first, because I thought [what they were proposing] was a massive undertaking, and I wasn't sure whether the city of Toronto or Metro, at the time, would want to proceed with it. But they were very persistent."

"At this point, in early 1998, Al and I didn't know what we were doing, really," McCamus says. "We didn't understand how the committee system worked. We were gaining our sea legs as the ship set sail. And we fell down a few times."

The pair quickly gained an understanding of *realpolitik*. "Suppose you were a councillor and inclined to oppose the barrier, what would you do?" McCamus asks rhetorically. "You'd sit back and wait to see what the Urban Environment and Development [UED] committee did. If it killed the idea in the first round, then that's great. It's dead. You don't have to publicly declare that you oppose a controversial suicide prevention project. It can be blamed on the UED's councillors. You get what you want, but don't take any blame for it. Or, if UED asks the Works department for a report, and the report comes back negative — for example, they say there's no evidence barriers save lives — that's also good for an opponent. A councillor can say, 'I didn't stop it. The Works department said it's useless. City staff didn't recommend it.' We didn't know or understand any of that until much later. We were learning through trial and error. Over time, we got better at it. We were complete political novices in a forum led by veteran politicians with years or decades of experience."

Birney and McCamus left Prue's office chastened but with assurance of his support.

Their next meeting in January was with the Dutch-born deputy mayor, Case Ootes (pronounced "Otis"), who the *Globe and Mail* once described as "in person an amiable and obviously intelligent man [but] in public he's a stiff."

Ootes, who represented the East York ward, was well aware of the viaduct's reputation. He not only applauded Birney and McCamus's efforts, after the meeting he wrote to acting-medical officer of health, Sheela Basrur, asking if fencing the viaduct would reduce the overall number of suicides in Toronto.

Her reply focused on the period 1990 to 1996, when the viaduct had almost as many suicides as all other bridges in Toronto combined. "Something like six and a half per year at the viaduct, seven or eight per year at all the other bridges," McCamus recalls. "Her data didn't include the year 1997, when the viaduct suicides shot up to seventeen, probably a result of Kruze and Au Yeung's well-publicized deaths and the ensuing notoriety. Her letter concluded that "there is good reason to believe that at least some individuals would not die if prevented from jumping at that location."

The letter was a godsend that Birney and McCamus used in all future discussions with councillors.

The First News Conference

The first significant development in the campaign followed a mid-February meeting with high-profile downtown councillor Jack Layton, who would later become leader of the federal New Democratic Party. It was clear from the outset that he was fully on board. He proposed holding a news conference the following weekend, on a Sunday. "It's usually a slow news day," he said, suggesting the event would give the media something to report.

AN OFFICER REMEMBERS

Superintendent Maher, who is now eighty-five, once witnessed a suicide on the viaduct. One year, he received a call that someone looked like he was going to jump. "I happened to be on the road, and I was close, and I responded," he remembers. "The young lad was on the south side. He just got off his bicycle [and was sitting] on the parapet."

As Maher stopped his car and started to cross the street to help, the young man got off the parapet and looked as if he was about to get on his bike. "I said to myself, oh, thank goodness," Maher says. "The next thing, he jumped up, back on the parapet, and I shouted, 'oh, hey, hold on.' But, boom, he jumped."

Maher later received a call from the mother, who wanted him to show her exactly where her son had died. "I met her below the parapet, and I pointed out the spot, and she put some flowers there. That impact, it never goes away."

The project was ideal for Layton, who had positioned himself as an ally and spokesperson for the powerless and disenfranchised. It would help marginalized and voiceless people and would be difficult to oppose politically without making the opponent appear to be heartless. "We were very pleased to have his support," McCamus says.

On February 22, 1998, Birney, McCamus, Councillor Layton, Dr. Paul Links, and police superintendent Aidan Maher fronted a news conference in a committee room on the second floor of Toronto's Metro Hall. As was his practice, Maher arrived in full dress uniform. "It tends to make an impression," he says.

As Layton had predicted, a throng of reporters showed up.

He told them he would request that the UED committee consider the barrier issue at its next meeting in March.

Superintendent Maher said that a fence should be constructed, as a minimum, to block people from jumping onto the Don Valley Parkway or

A SURVIVOR'S TESTIMONY

"For the news conference, we invited as many SSO (Schizophrenia Society of Ontario) volunteers as we could to fill up the committee room," says McCamus. "We wanted the media to see that families of the mentally ill were concerned and supporting this cause."

SSO volunteer Ravi Sarin was there with his mother, Marilyn Sarin. Marilyn was a former nurse and chief organizer of Walk the World for Schizophrenia Research, an annual SSO walkathon in Toronto.

Ravi told the reporters that when he was a teenager and first diagnosed with schizophrenia, he was feeling lost and hopeless. He went to the viaduct, stood at its precipice, and agonized about killing himself. But when he thought of how much that would hurt his family, he decided to go home instead. Ravi's story appeared the next day on the front page of the *Globe and Mail*.

the Bayview Extension, the two highways running underneath the viaduct. Bodies had landed on the highways, and on cars, he said.

Dr. Links answered that pesky, ubiquitous question that dogged the fence proposal whenever it was raised: Won't people just jump somewhere else?

"If you look at what's been done in other jurisdictions," he said, "at the Eiffel Tower or the Empire State Building or [the active volcano] Mount Mihara in Japan, where they've done things to remove access to these sites, they've had a lot of success."

During a question period, "Al and I noticed that whenever we said something slightly dramatic," recalls McCamus, "the reporters would start scribbling in their notebooks. For example, a reporter asked us how much the fence on the viaduct would cost? Al said that the fence in Glens Falls had cost about a hundred thousand dollars. I added, 'It's been paid for with the blood, sweat, and tears of three hundred families.' Then all the reporters' heads dropped as they wrote furiously. It was our first lesson in how to speak in quotable soundbites."

At the end of the formal part of the conference, the speakers attempted to leave. But reporters crowded around them and peppered them with more questions.

"Another lesson we learned is that reporters come with certain requirements," says McCamus. "This was a story about suicide and prevention. The reporters really wanted to interview someone who had survived a suicide or prevented one. I made a mental note in the back of my mind: We need to have families of someone who jumped when we speak to the media."

Although the conference was a media success, behind the scenes not everyone was happy. Birney, at the time, considered himself a capital-C Conservative. He counted several elected members of the Harris government as close friends.

After the news conference, more than one told him it had been a mistake. "Now it looks like your project is Jack Layton's pet project," they told him. Enough conservatives on city council disliked the NDP's Layton so much they might vote against the barrier simply to deny a political opponent a win, they said. A couple of the councillors told him: "Look, we want to support your bridge project, but we don't want to be supporting a Layton project."

As a result, Birney started having second thoughts about the wisdom of the news conference. Did it really work for the good of the project or not? "We've got to get the support of everybody, no matter what their political stripe," he ultimately said.

Support from the Right

Birney's concerns proved unfounded; in the years ahead, two of the staunchest supporters of the campaign were the most conservative members of council: Case Ootes and budget chief Tom Jakobek (although the latter would sour on the campaign for a short period of time).

Jakobek was an interesting character. Born in 1959, he was a brilliant and ambitious student. In 1980, he was elected to the Toronto District School Board, the youngest public school–trustee in Ontario's history. Two years later he was elected to city council, becoming, at age twenty-one, the youngest ever to accomplish that feat. In 1990, he became budget chief, a position he held for the next ten years, during which he delivered nine consecutive budgets that had no tax increases.

A steadfast right-winger and ally of Mel Lastman, he had an apparent empathy for people in crisis, having volunteered when he was a student to answer phones at the crisis line in what was then called Toronto East General Hospital. When on council, he would often drive Olivia Chow, a left-wing councillor and wife of Jack Layton, home during the winter months, because she couldn't safely ride her bicycle in the snow.

A Breakthrough

True to his word, Jack Layton wrote to the Urban Environment and Development Committee, asking it to discuss suicide prevention measures for the viaduct. On March 23, 1998, the UED committee debated the viaduct issue for the first time ever. McCamus and Superintendent Maher attended the meeting, along with Dr. Isaac Sakinofsky, a professor in the

UNFRIENDLY COVERAGE

At this time, opposition to the barrier was not led by politicians but by several journalists.

Columnist John Barber of the the *Globe and Mail* wrote that "Noble Fight May Bring Chain-link Epidemic."

Globe arts critic John Bentley Mays worried that a "Sad History Mars Glorious Span," an over-the-top appraisal of the Bloor Viaduct as an engineering masterpiece unworthy of chain-link fences.

Both columnists' concerns had to do with aesthetics: An ugly fence would destroy a beautiful and important monument.

Not so for *Toronto Star* columnist Rosie DiManno. She simply called a barrier of any kind "a waste of money."

"There was also opposition in letters to the editor and, of course, on radio call-in shows that attract lonely, angry people who want to be heard complaining," McCamus says.

Department of Psychiatry at the University of Toronto, who had researched and written extensively about suicide.

His expertise emanated from an assignment he took on following the death of Kenneth Au Yeung. The Council on Suicide Prevention — a group of mental health professionals in Toronto — asked Sakinofsky to prepare a comprehensive literature review of all the academic studies on "suicide magnets," which he presented at the March 23 UED committee meeting.

Sakinofsky urged the councillors to take immediate action. "What is important," he said, "is to change the perception of the viaduct from a bridge of death to a place of light and life and celebration, a place where no one would ever think of committing suicide." He referenced a jazz festival held on the Duke Ellington Bridge.

The presentations had their effect. The committee directed the Works department to meet with SSO volunteers, research prevention strategies, and report back. It was a tremendous step forward, Birney said at the time.

These were the early days of their campaign, but Birney and McCamus were starting to believe that "all the stars were aligning in favour of this project," McCamus says. "There were so many strokes of luck: meeting Karen Letofsky was extremely fortunate. Getting the early support of the deputy mayor was a lucky break. Getting such enthusiastic support from Layton was an unexpected boost from obscurity to front page news."

Then came another gift. "Of all the bureaucrats working at Metro Hall, we got Les Kelman as the manager of the project during the research and design phase," McCamus says. "He was an open-minded, affable, highly professional engineer who seemed personally interested in seeing the barrier come to fruition."

Kelman doesn't remember being surprised at the retiree and student he had to work with. "It wasn't like they had invented the issue, it was already within the public domain, in the newspapers, in the media," he says. "So, even if they were slightly unusual or different from the people I had been used to dealing with, there was no escaping that it was a serious issue."

Kelman had transferred from Toronto's traffic control centre to work in construction, which he says traffic people consider "the dark side." He was curious to find out what construction was like, so he accepted a parallel short-term transfer about the time the barrier issue became a political hot potato.

"We had to scramble to research what the issue was," he says. "The trouble is, when you start a literature search into all of this, ninety percent of 'people jumping from bridges' deals with damage to the body when it hits the water. There is very little that we found that would help us understand what was going on [at the viaduct]. But we kept plugging away. Very quickly, we had reached a conclusion that the issue was legitimate, and the concerns were legitimate, and the outcomes were almost predictable, to a certain extent."

"What also likely helped," says McCamus, "was that Kelman was an acquaintance of Superintendent Maher."

Indeed, he was. A Scottish-born engineer, Kelman, who retired from the city's transportation department in 2007, played soccer with Maher, an Irishman, on weekends.

THE POWER OF PERSONAL STORIES

Of the hundreds of families that had lost a loved one to the Bloor Viaduct, only three came forward to help Birney and McCamus lobby for a barrier: the parents of Kenneth Au Yeung, Gary and Teresa Kruze, and Ray and Mary Doucette. Vee Ledson, the partner of writer H.S. Bhabra, who would take his life from the viaduct in 2000, also volunteered her assistance.

Birney saw something of himself in Ray and Mary, who would celebrate their fiftieth wedding anniversary in 2007. "They were a retired couple that had tried to help their son deal with mental illness," he said. "Then they had the traumatic shock and anguish of his suicide. The big difference is their son died and mine didn't. But I felt connected to them nonetheless."

In June 1998, the Doucettes spoke in public for the first time about their thirty-six-year-old son's death a year earlier, at a meeting of the Urban Environment and Development Committee chaired by Joe Pantalone.

"Why did my son choose the Bloor Street Viaduct?" Ray asked rhetorically. "It does the job. You won't be maimed or crippled [afterward]. You are going to die. There are people behind us who visit their children at psychiatric hospitals," motioning to SSO members who had come to the meeting to support the campaign, "but because of the Bloor Viaduct, my wife and I visit our son at the cemetery."

In the coming years, whenever there was a public meeting of one of the city's various committees, Mary was there, sitting in front of the councillors, asking them to spare other mothers what she had had to endure. If they were going to say no, they would have to look into the face of a grieving mother, see her anguish, and turn her down.

"Her daughter, Colleen, told me she was amazed how her demure, quiet-spoken mother became a confident, outspoken advocate for the Bloor Viaduct barrier," says Michael McCamus. "That was the power that she and her husband held over council. They wielded it with humility and caution, grace and judiciousness."

"The Doucettes were our secret weapon," Birney often said. "If we needed them to come to a meeting to personalize the impact of a death at the viaduct, one or both of them would come."

Some years later, Joe Pantalone acknowledged the importance of Ray Doucette's presentation at the 1998 meeting, at which his committee voted to fund the Veil. "It was hard to argue when you came face-to-face with people who lost a son or a daughter," he said. "When they stare you in the eye, it's hard to say, 'Go away, lives are not worth spending money on.'"

Soon after meeting Birney and McCamus, Kelman made it clear that he personally endorsed their campaign. "He read the materials that we and Karen and Sakinofsky presented, which we really appreciated," McCamus says.

Kelman was tasked to write an "options analysis" for the UED committee so it could choose a path forward. Even before the committee had requested a report, Kelman and colleagues in the Works department had conducted research on different barriers and their costs. This was in reply to Deputy Mayor Ootes, who had requested this information following his meeting with Birney and McCamus in January 1998.

They contacted suppliers of off-the-rack fences and nets. They found that the cost of a chain-link fence ranged from $450,000 to $750,000. The Works department, or perhaps Kelman himself, set the budget for the barrier at $1.5 million; they had simply doubled the $750,000, knowing how costs can quickly escalate. Their ballpark estimate seemed reasonable and logical for the kind of structure being contemplated at the time, but it later turned out to be grossly inaccurate for building a one-of-a-kind barrier on an eighty-year-old steel-and-concrete structure spanning half a kilometre over two highways, a railway, electricity lines, gas lines, and a major river.

"The issue of the budget has been a sore point with me ever since," says Kelman. "The person who won the competition [Dereck Revington] and committed to do it for one and a half million probably knew all the way along that it wasn't possible."

On June 15, 1998, the UED committee heard deputations from Birney, McCamus, Karen Letofsky, Dr. Sakinofsky, Dr. Links, Dr. Robin Richards (head of orthopaedic surgery at St. Michael's Hospital), and bereaved parents Ray and Mary Doucette.

Dr. Richards had operated on survivors of suicide attempts in the subway, as well as survivors of falls from the Bloor Viaduct (and the Gerrard Street Bridge, which is also over the Don Valley but is much shorter). He estimated the initial surgery on survivors from a viaduct jump was $100,000. He said the estimate did not include the cost of rehabilitation, disability pensions, mobility aids, or lost productivity.

At the end of the presentations, the UED committee approved a Works department recommendation to hold a barrier design competition, with a $1.5 million budget, and send the matter to council. "If you recommend this to council and it declines, then I think council is guilty of euthanasia or council-assisted suicide," Ray Doucette said on the way out the door.

He had no need to worry. On July 8, council greenlit the contest to find a functional and heritage-sensitive barrier. Budget chief Jakobek said the $1.5 million would come out of a corporate contingency account.

REPORT CARD

Michael McCamus once described the teaching style of three of the councillors: "Jack Layton was like the cool history teacher who knows everything about everything and wants to share what he knows with you.

"Michael Prue was like a very friendly, energetic science teacher who wanted to get the things done we needed to get done and then go outside for some fun.

"Case Ootes was like a strict principal. You had to be on your guard around him. He was quiet, like Clint Eastwood, but a good listener. He'd occasionally ask a question that showed he was interested and trying to understand."

Birney and McCamus were ecstatic. In just over six months, their campaign seemed to have succeeded: A barrier was imminent. If only that had turned out to be true. They didn't know it at the time, but many obstacles still lay ahead.

7

The Black Dogs

On March 12, 1998, John Bentley Mays, the *Globe and Mail*'s visual arts critic, wrote a column about the viaduct entitled "Sad History Mars Glorious Span." In fewer than a thousand words, Mays both lamented the bridge's dark history as a suicide magnet and lauded its practical purpose and stunning elegance.

After praising its creators' foresight in adding a subway level many decades before it was needed, he turned his attention to what he called their "remarkable esthetic judgments [that] have received less attention and praise. Conscious of the beauty of the valley, they provided sidewalks and overlooks, offering strollers high and unobstructed views of this wild, wide ravine carved by runoff into the otherwise crowded core of the metropolis."

If the city installed high chain-link fencing, he argued, it would deface the viaduct, which is a designated structure under the Ontario Heritage Act, in unacceptable ways. "[It] joins steel and concrete, modernity and Classicism, the triumphant celebration of 20th-century engineering and the recollection of the age-old art of bridge building into a unity that has been justly admired since the day it was constructed. If barriers must be raised on it to foil people wishing to hurl themselves to certain death, we can only hope that the designers of such fences will respect the nobility and grandeur of this Canadian masterpiece of engineering art."

Mays should not be perceived as having a callous attitude toward people struggling with their mental health: quite the opposite.

Three years before writing his column, he had published *In the Jaws of the Black Dogs: A Memoir of Depression*, using the phrase Winston Churchill had coined to describe his own battle with despair. Describing a lifelong struggle with depression, Mays said in an interview words that many jumpers from the viaduct would likely have understood all too well: "Absolutely I live with fear. I never know when it's going to come back. I don't know why it comes back. The Black Dogs just come out of the forest whenever they want to and try to trap me once again. That sense of being part of the world is lost and you experience the desolation of being nowhere and nobody."

An influential voice in Toronto, Mays had set the tone for the design competition that would kickstart a few months later: yes to a barrier but no to a chain-link fence. It was advice the jurors charged with deciding the winning design heard loud and clear.

This Is How Committees Are Formed?

On March 31, 1998, a "working team" of Les Kelman, Al Birney, Michael McCamus, Karen Letofsky, and Dr. Isaac Sakinofsky came together for the first time. The meetings would become frequent over the months and years ahead. City council would later call them "the Bloor Viaduct Project Steering Committee (PSC)," as suggested by Kelman.

The meetings took place in a large conference room on the sixteenth floor of Metro Hall. It boasted "a giant window overlooking the public square and the theatre district below," McCamus says. "It was a gorgeous view. Al and I loved being in that room."

In April, Kelman invited John Blumenson of the Toronto Historical Board to join the PSC because the board was entitled to consult on any changes to historic sites in the city. Birney and McCamus were initially defensive and guarded around Blumenson because of what they had seen as interference by the historical conservationists in Washington, D.C. In private, never in public, Birney dubbed it the "hysterical board" for what he felt was its overreaction to any possible changes to the viaduct.

It turned out they were wrong. "Thankfully, John Blumenson was a perfectly congenial and reasonable person, whom we got to like," McCamus says.

At the PSC's first meeting, however, their relationship with Blumenson got off to a rough start. Birney showed Blumenson photos of the chain-link fence on New York State's Glen Street Bridge.

"I think we can do much better than that," Blumenson said.

"Come on. You've said no to everything," Birney snapped. "Don't you have to say yes to something sometime?"

Birney's annoyance with Blumenson would build up over the next few meetings. "At that time, we were expecting the city would buy a kind of

THAT'S WHY YOU'RE CALLED VOLUNTEERS

"At times, Al offended the other Bloor Viaduct Project Steering Committee members by suggesting they weren't working as hard as he and I were. They didn't like that," McCamus says. "He was a very good man but often became frustrated that the wheels of government took longer than he thought they should."

At one gathering, Birney said, "Every time you call a meeting, we have to drive down from Scarborough, burning up our own time and gas. I'm sitting around a table with people who are making six-figure salaries for all I know. I'm a volunteer and a pensioner. I don't get paid for this."

Letofsky and Sakinofsky bristled at this comment. Sakinofsky said, "Al, we don't get paid either. We're taking time away from work for this." He was referencing his role at the Clarke Institute of Psychiatry (about to be renamed the Centre for Addiction and Mental Health) as director of the High [Suicide] Risk Consultation Clinic, which specialized in support for high-risk patients; Letofsky took time off from her role as executive director of the Distress Centres.

"Al's outburst didn't make a good impression on them," McCamus says. "Nobody was forcing us to do this."

off-the-rack barrier, not require a one-of-a-kind solution," McCamus says. The two volunteers did not understand or support the arguments by Mays and the Toronto Historical Board that a barrier absolutely had to be aesthetic as well as functional. They would soon change their stance.

The two men were aware that their off-the-rack solution would likely not work for practical reasons, never mind aesthetic concerns. At a previous interaction with engineer Mike Chung of the Works department, Chung had told them that "whatever you put up there will have to withstand the ice and wind loads." Neither had thought of that. Chung explained that you couldn't just bolt a chain-link fence to the sidewalk because it wouldn't be able to withstand the weight of winter ice and the power of the wind ripping through the Don Valley.

Despite this warning, Birney and McCamus advocated for their proposal out of a belief that it was the only affordable solution. Anything more complicated would likely cost too much and could force the politicians to abandon the entire project; they desperately wanted a functional barrier, even an ugly one.

Blumenson kept fighting for his vision, and as he did, Birney and McCamus came to regard him as an ally. They learned that others on his board didn't want any barrier at all, but he was committed to finding a design that met everyone's requirements.

His insistence on an aesthetic solution gained support when Jane Perdue joined the PSC in June. A public art coordinator for the city since 1991, she had also worked with other municipalities on developing public art policies and public art master plans. Together, Blumenson and Perdue won the day: There would be no chain-link fence.

The Process Begins

Kelman was determined to elicit design proposals for a barrier. He had no intention of proceeding slowly. To develop and manage the process, he retained two consultants: Stephen G. McLaughlin (no relation to the author) and Leslie Coates.

McLaughlin was a highly respected senior architect. He had left his practice for a period of time to act as senior policy adviser to Mayor David Crombie in the early seventies, then became Toronto's first Commissioner of Planning and Development and co-authored Toronto's first urban design manual, *On Building Downtown*.

Coates was a young consultant. She went on to become a manager of special projects for the City of Toronto's Parks, Forestry and Recreation before retiring.

"The fact that the Works department hired someone as impressive as McLaughlin showed it wanted the best and the brightest to make the project come to fruition," says McCamus. "It was a very positive sign."

The terms of reference for the competition, which would be overseen by the PSC, were driven by Coates. "It was her baby, and she did her job extremely well," McCamus says. McLaughlin's job was to be a go-between with the architectural firms (at least one member of a team had to be a licenced engineer or architect in Ontario). As an architect, he would be more than capable of answering any questions they had about the contest and could troubleshoot any problems that arose during the competition.

With the assistance of Perdue, Coates drew up twelve criteria that applicants had to keep in mind, including the following:

- It would need to prevent people from jumping; nets would not be a solution, as they could be cut or tampered with, and the police had no interest in disentangling people out of them.
- It had to respect the architectural integrity of the existing viaduct.
- The design should aspire to be a piece of public art.
- It should aim to improve the experience of users of the bridge, including pedestrians, cyclists, motorists.
- It should minimize the impact on views to and from the bridge.
- In no way should it memorialize the suicides at the viaduct.

In other words, there should be no references to names, dates, identities, or circumstances of previous suicides on display.

This last point was especially important to suicide prevention experts Karen Letofsky and Isaac Sakinofsky, who felt certain that any kind of memorializing would lead to copycat suicides. Memorials could provide an incentive to a troubled, vulnerable person to kill themself at a site at which their suicide might be remembered or even honoured.

Kelman had an ad placed in several publications, including the *Globe and Mail* and the *Toronto Star*, on July 11, with submissions for stage one of the competition due by July 27. Entries would not require detailed drawings but, rather, the architects' initial design ideas and how they would meet the criteria. Sixteen top architectural firms participated in stage one.

In May, Les Kelman convinced the city to create a seven-person jury, which would be tasked with deciding the winner of the design competition that would be announced in a few months.

In addition to himself, the other jurors were Al Birney, Karen Letofsky, Dr. Sakinofsky, Carole Stimmell of the Toronto Historical Board (which would be renamed Heritage Toronto as of January 1, 2000), architect Adrian DiCastri, a founding partner of architectsAlliance and an award-winning architect, and architect Ellis Galea Kirkland, who had a master's in urban design from Harvard. The latter three had recently joined the Bloor Viaduct Project Steering Committee. Kirkland would later become a tragic figure in a most ironic way.

McCamus was not a member but acted as an adviser to Birney.

The seven jurors, who were also referred to as the Barrier Design Selection Committee, met on July 30 and designated four entries for stage two: Brown + Storey Architects; Dereck Revington Studio; E.R.A. Architects; and Montgomery Sisam Architects. "I was impressed with how quickly the process was proceeding, especially for a local government initiative," says McCamus. "I attribute that to Les Kelman."

The finalists were invited to city hall on August 5 for the announcement. One in particular impressed Birney and McCamus. "Dereck Revington came up to us and shook our hands," says McCamus. "He said, 'I think this is really great, what you guys are doing.' He was very excited about the project."

But Revington didn't have much time to waste with niceties: The deadline for stage two (a detailed barrier design) was August 27.

All finalists met the deadline. They didn't have long to wait to find out if they had won. In keeping with its rapid pace of play, the seven-juror panel met again on August 28 to decide the winner.

Dereck Revington's Luminous Veil, which was designed with "the help of two former students at the time, Geoffrey Thün and Kathy Velikov," he says, received six enthusiastic votes; E.R.A.'s design garnered one, from Carole Stimmell of the Toronto Historical Board. The highly respected conservationist (in 2002, she would receive a Queen Elizabeth II Golden Jubilee Medal) said she liked it largely due to the fact that it included artistic bronze maple leaves that would be posted on the viaduct, showing important historical milestones in the history of the structure, for example, Mayor Tommy Church turning the sod on January 16, 1915, to begin construction of the viaduct, its official opening on October 18, 1918, and so on.

THE VEIL EXPLAINED

Kathy Velikov and Geoffrey Thün, who collaborated during the design competition with Revington, their former architecture professor at the University of Waterloo, later incorporated his conception of the Luminous Veil on their website.

"The Luminous Veil is conceived as a tremulous spatial fabric strung against the sky and running from bank to bank on both sides of the bridge. Tensioned between a horizontal 'V' truss (suspended sixteen feet above the deck) and the balustrade, its oscillating double skin holds the fatal threshold between the sidewalk and the valley below. It is designed both as a deterrent to suicide, and as a kinesthetic field of reflection. The parallel veils on both sides of the bridge create a lightly contained space on the deck, giving it volume and definition through a tracery of shimmering vertical lines superimposed on sprung bow-spring masts, which fold into the valley beyond."

It was a component that seemed tailor-made to appeal to the historical board. (It was later discovered, however, that the cost of creating the maple leaves were not part of the budget submitted.) The fears that Birney and McCamus had felt when the historical board was given a seat on the jury, that it would advocate for design over prevention, seemed to have come true.

"How could she not have voted for the Veil?" Birney asked. "It was the only one that met all of the requirements. It was by far the best proposal," as everyone on the jury but Stimmel agreed.

Despite Stimmell's dissenting vote, on September 8, 1998, Kelman presented the Luminous Veil to the Urban Environment and Development (UED) committee as the jury's official choice for the barrier. Although not a member of the committee, Jack Layton attended and spoke in support of the Veil.

The response from some of Layton's fellow NDP councillors was far from positive. Pam McConnell, a left-leaning downtown representative, said, "To me it looks like a cage. I don't know anything about architecture." Another left-winger, longtime North York councillor Howard Moscoe, likened the Veil, with its ten thousand high-tension wires, to a giant egg slicer.

Suffice to say, the UED committee did not find the design compelling. They demonstrated a lot of skepticism and confusion. They were concerned that the Toronto Historical Board had voted for a different approach.

In typical government fashion, a "working team" of four councillors was formed to study the design and report directly to council at its next meeting, on October 1, 1998. The UED committee also decided to hold an open house so residents could examine the architect's drawings before council would vote.

Birney Loses His Cool

Al Birney did not take these developments well. He had expected, perhaps somewhat naively, that his campaign was close to a successful completion. Instead, additional meetings had been scheduled, offering opponents more chances to delay or terminate the project.

"Delay seemed to be a strategy at city hall," says McCamus. "It was a way to avoid making a decision. To say Al and I were frustrated was an understatement."

Birney perceived that councillors McConnell and Layton, rather than helping to push the project forward, were contributing to the delays. He took his frustration out on Layton in a hallway after the UED meeting had concluded. It was an unfortunate decision.

"Jack, what's going on? I've been calling you dozens and dozens of times, and you didn't get back to me."

Layton replied in a businesslike tone, "Who did you talk to in my office?"

"One of your little girls in there," referring to Layton's assistant, Monica Tang.

"They are not little girls," Layton said, raising his voice. "She's a master's student!"

Birney knew he had made a mistake. He toned it down somewhat. "Why didn't you get back to me?"

Layton lost his temper. "I was in surgery, if you have to know everything!" Later, it was revealed that Layton had had a hernia repaired at a private medical clinic. It became an issue when he became the federal NDP leader, because his party opposed private health clinics.

Layton then confronted Birney on an exaggeration. "I track my calls. You haven't been calling me 'dozens and dozens of times.'" The latter was said in a sarcastic tone.

As Layton walked away in frustration, Birney muttered under his breath, "Surgery? Did they take one or two, Jack?" meaning his testicles.

The encounter left McCamus concerned. It was not the way to deal with one of your most important supporters.

Biking in a Tuxedo

McConnell and Layton held their open house at Metro Toronto Reference Library on September 28, 1998.

Not many people showed up. Layton arrived on his bicycle, wearing a tuxedo from a previous event. There were display boards in an open area of the library, and people could mill about looking at drawings of the Veil and ask Revington questions.

"I don't think there's any civilians here," Birney said to McCamus. "Fifteen, maybe." Most of the attendees were from the city or Revington's design team, or were members of the PSC. Kelman was there and not in a good mood toward McCamus. "I had pissed him off because I'd issued a news release about the open house without consulting him or Layton and McConnell," McCamus says.

"This is not a meeting of the Schizophrenia Society," Kelman said, sternly. "It's a meeting for the constituents of councillors McConnell and Layton and the members of the public."

"We're members of the public," McCamus snipped. Kelman walked away.

Days later, Birney, McCamus, and Revington sat down with the historical board's directors to persuade them to support the Veil. To their relief, the board gave its approval. They liked the design process, they said, because it reinforced the precedent that heritage conservationists should be consulted on these kinds of projects.

That support likely helped convince city council, on October 1, to vote unanimously in favour of the Luminous Veil.

It seemed to Birney and McCamus that victory was imminent. But as they were quickly learning, politics doesn't always follow a predictable script.

8

The Copycat Question

On February 25, 1998, regional coroner for Toronto, Dr. William Lucas, announced he would convene an inquest into the death of Kenneth Au Yeung.

It's possible his decision was influenced by two recent full-capacity parent meetings held at St. Michael's Choir School. On both occasions, parents expressed their anger and frustration at the school, the Toronto Catholic School Board, and the Toronto Police Service. All three institutions were facing ongoing criticism for their role in Au Yeung's suicide.

"During the first meeting — on Dec. 17, six days after the [1997] suicide — parents crowded into the school cafeteria. Instead of answers, they were given a seminar on suicide counselling and bereavement," *Maclean's* reported in a February article, "Death of a Choirboy."

They were told by Michael O'Flanagan, superintendent for the Metropolitan Separate School Board, that the authorities were handling the matter and reports would be made public in due time. "They listened patiently — but eventually one father with two sons in the school rose and started directing uncomfortable questions at O'Flanagan. According to sources at the meeting, the father wanted to know who was responsible for the tragedy and said the parents had a right to the information."

On January 18, another meeting was held with parents, this time in the school's auditorium. It lasted more than ninety minutes. Superintendent

O'Flanagan once again attended, this time accompanied by a board lawyer, *Maclean's* reported: "Again, the agenda featured a long lecture on grieving and bereavement. But the parents were not there for an abstract seminar. They had stopped grieving and had moved well down the road to anger: they wanted cold hard facts.

"When a mother rose and said she, like all the parents, simply wanted official confirmation of what had happened, and who was responsible, the crowd applauded. O'Flanagan tried to mollify her by saying the coroner and the police were looking into matters. At that, another father stood up and said, 'Is this a meeting of the board or a meeting of the parents?' He was applauded as well," *Maclean's* wrote.

School principal John Ryall did not attend the meeting but afterward denied that the school was "trying to keep parents in the dark. 'Are there a whole series of things that the school knows and is covering up? Not to my knowledge,' he said. 'I'm not Bill Clinton. There's no conspiracy of silence here that I'm aware of.'"

The inquest began on June 17, led by counsel to the coroner, Al O'Marra, a lawyer with the ministry of the Attorney General. He would later be appointed a judge of the Superior Court of Justice in and for Ontario.

During the next seventeen days, O'Marra would examine every aspect of the events leading up to, and culminating in, Au Yeung's suicide.

A MOTHER'S PAIN

On July 3, at the inquest into her son's death, Au Yeung's mother, Catherine, told the jury in a hushed voice she believed her son would still be alive if his parents had been present during the interrogation by his school's principal and off-duty police officer Downer. She also addressed the fact that the school's administrators would not let her son call home. "If it was your child, you would want to be there."

Maclean's would describe her testimony as a "wrenching moment."

That he chose to jump off the Bloor Viaduct, as had Martin Kruze, raised an important question. When the inquest had been announced five months earlier, Toronto's deputy chief coroner, Dr. James Cairns, said that, among matters, it would try to determine "whether there was a 'copycat' element in Kenneth's suicide."

Dr. Isaac Sakinofsky addressed that question in his testimony on July 6, a few days before the city placed the newspaper and magazine ads calling for barrier design proposals.

To Sakinofsky, who was appearing as an expert witness on suicides, especially among the young, the answer was abundantly clear. He told the five-person jury that the extensive media coverage of Martin Kruze's death likely led to Au Yeung's decision to kill himself at the same location.

The media needed to be careful about how it reported suicides because of the copycat or contagion effect, he said. Then he went one big step further.

"We believe that one ought to keep suicides that happen out of the media," the head of the suicide studies program at Toronto's Clarke Institute of Psychiatry advised. "If they really have to be publicized, they should be moved to the back page — not glorified." He knew it was a proposition the media would likely not accept, but he wanted to make the statement, nonetheless.

Although Sakinofsky acknowledged that other factors contributed to Au Yeung's decision to end his life — especially the hardline questioning the young man was subjected to by school officials and off-duty Toronto police Constable Christopher Downer — Sakinofsky urged the jury to recommend that the media develop stricter guidelines for reporting on suicides.

The Werther Effect

At the core of Sakinofsky's presentation were two theories, both of which were widely accepted by the suicidology discipline: the Werther and Papageno effects.

In 1845, American psychiatrist Amariah Brigham, founder and first editor of the *American Journal of Insanity*, stated, "No fact is better

THE MEDIA RESPOND

On July 11, Don Sellar, the *Toronto Star*'s ombudsman (as the role was called at the time), wrote a response to what he perceived as criticism of the way the media reports suicides. "With respect, it seems the media messengers have taken an undeserved rap here," he began. "Was there not an overwhelmingly public interest in the two high-profile suicides? Au Yeung went to a school that relies partly on public funds. Surely, any police role in solving school problems is a matter for open discussion.

"As for Kruze, his suicide came three days after Gordon Stuckless, the man convicted of abusing him and 25 others, got what many said was a lenient sentence of two years less a day. Did Kruze's death rate only an inside page?

"And, by the way, do experts in what's called 'suicidology' think that potential suicides only read Page 1 and won't see suicide articles buried deep in the paper?"

Sellar went on to note that editors must find an "overriding public interest" before they report a death as a suicide. "[However], it's also fair to say news stories about the two suicide cases helped prod civic leaders into considering safety barriers at the Bloor St. Viaduct. With censorship, would there be any debate?"

He was not alone in his opinion.

The following year, Doris Anderson, the highly respected journalist who was serving as chair of the Ontario Press Council, said the recommendation on media guidelines from the Au Yeung inquest was "unnecessary" because its members have "generally shown they are responsible and sensitive in dealing with this subject."

The council added, "The press does not report suicides unless they are clearly newsworthy and did not see the need for authorities to withhold information about them."

established in science, than that suicide is often committed from imitation. A single paragraph may suggest suicide to twenty persons. Some particulars of the act, or expressions, seize the imagination, and the disposition to repeat it, in a moment of morbid excitement, proves irresistible."

In 1897, sociologist Émile Durkheim, wrote in *Suicide: A Study in Sociology*, "No fact is more readily transmissible by contagion than suicide."

These blunt assertions were likely influenced by a 1774 epistolary novel by Johann Wolfgang von Goethe, *The Sorrows of Young Werther*. Goethe's novel recounts the tragic story of Werther, a young artist who falls hopelessly in love with Charlotte, a happily married woman. In this overwrought romantic tale, Werther kills himself with a pistol after failing to win her love.

The novel, which was inspired by the suicide of the teenage English poet Thomas Chatterton, introduced the concept of the "romantic suicide," Dr. Alexandra Pitman, an associate professor at University College London, wrote in the *British Journal of Psychiatry*, in 2015.

Eighteenth-century authors "embellished these men as romantic outcasts, triumphing over death through fearless individualism to achieve immortality in heaven," Pitman wrote. "Such myths still persist today, exemplified in journalists' responses to the suicides of artists such as Kitaj, Kirchner, Rothko and Van Gogh. Glorifying their deaths by wreathing them in martyrdom is a dangerous practice. Awareness of the damage wreaked by propagation of these myths is the starting point for challenging them."

Following publication of *The Sorrows of Young Werther*, many young European men began wearing blue jackets, yellow trousers, and open-necked shirts, in emulation of Werther's chosen dress style. More disturbing, however, were reports that a significant number of young men took their own lives, although whether this actually happened on any large scale has been questioned in recent years. The perceived problem, however, was such that the book was banned in several jurisdictions because of the fear of social contagion. Goethe, who himself had suicidal thoughts, became convinced that some people believed they should "imitate a novel like this in real life and, in any case, shoot themselves; and what occurred at first among a few took place later among the general public."

NO SUICIDE IS BEAUTIFUL

One of the most famous examples of a "romanticized" suicide (a death made to seem glamorous) is the case of Evelyn McHale, a twenty-three-year-old book-keeper who jumped off the eighty-sixth-floor observation deck of the Empire State Building on May 1, 1947. She plummeted 320 metres (1,050 feet) and landed on the roof of a United Nations Cadillac limousine, parked on 34th Street.

A photography student, Robert Wiles, heard the commotion Evelyn's fall caused and rushed outside with his camera. He was confronted with an ironic image. "The beautiful young woman was wearing [a gown], pearls and white gloves," artist Rebecca Paul wrote in a 2021 article, "The Wild and Dark History of the Empire State Building":

"With legs elegantly crossing at the ankles, her body lay morbidly lifeless but majestically intact as the car's metal folded around her like sheets framing her head and arm."

Wiles sold the picture he snapped to *Life* magazine, which ran it in the May 12, 1947, edition, subtitling it, "The most beautiful suicide." The image and the wording became famous and would be exploited in the future in many cultural forms.

That might not have happened if another picture had been taken of her body when it was moved. Various reports said her body essentially fell apart when it was lifted up. Her insides had become liquefied.

She had left her coat, a makeup kit full of family photographs, and a black pocketbook at the spot from where she had jumped. The book contained a note:

I don't want anyone in or out of my family to see any part of me. Could you destroy my body by cremation? I beg of you and my family — don't have any service for me or remembrance for me. My fiancé asked me to marry him in June. I don't think I would make a good wife for anybody. He is much better off without me. Tell my father I have too many of my mother's [negative] tendencies.

Her mother, who had left the family and then divorced Evelyn's father, suffered from untreated depression and other mental health challenges.

In the years since McHale's death, artists have been drawn to the image of her seemingly serene lifeless body. In 1962, Andy Warhol used the *Life* photo for an art piece he called *Suicide (Fallen Body)*. David Bowie recreated the image in the video of his 1993 single, "Jump They Say." To a lesser extent, Radiohead's Thom Yorke did the same for the band's 1995 video, "Street Spirit (Fade Out)." The punk band Saccharine Trust used the Wiles photo for the cover of its 1994 album, *Surviving You, Always*.

In a case of suspected suicide contagion, during a three-week period following McHale's death, four people jumped from the Empire State's observation deck. In response, management installed a ten-foot wire mesh fence around it and trained its guards to be on the lookout for people in distress.

In 1974, two hundred years after the novel was published, sociologist David Phillips, who was teaching at the State University of New York at Stony Brook at the time, coined the term the *Werther effect*, in an article he published in the *American Sociological Review*. "I was proud of the title I gave that paper," he says. "After the [Goethe] book came out, all sorts of people were said to be copying the fictional hero. And I said, 'Hey, let's see if this works in real life as well as in fiction.'"

In an abstract to his article, he said his research showed "that suicides increase immediately after a suicide story has been publicized in the newspapers in Britain and in the United States, 1947–1968. The more publicity devoted to a suicide story, the larger the rise in suicides thereafter. The rise in suicides after a story is restricted mainly to the area in which the story was publicized. The evidence indicates that the rise in suicides is due to the influence of suggestion on suicide, an influence not previously demonstrated on the national level of suicides."

In the years since Phillips dubbed suicide contagion as the Werther effect, the evidence supporting his thesis seems to have become more convincing.

"When Marilyn Monroe died in August 1962, with the cause listed as probable suicide, the nation reacted. In the months afterward, there was extensive news coverage, widespread sorrow and a spate of suicides," an August 2014 article in the *New York Times*'s "The Science Behind Suicide Contagion," reported. "According to one study, the suicide rate in the United States jumped by 12 percent compared with the same months in the previous year. People who kill themselves are already vulnerable, but publicity around another suicide appears to make a difference as they are considering

THE WRONG WORD

When the comedian Robin Williams ended his life in 2014, the *New York Daily News* ran a front-page photo of him looking gloomy. The huge headline read simply, "HANGED."

"The headline ... contravened the most basic recommendations of the World Health Organization and suicide prevention experts for how the media should cover suicide, including 'toning down' accounts, to avoid inspiring similar deaths," the *Washington Post* reported.

Suicides in the U.S. increased in the five months following the comedian's death, "especially among men ages 30 to 44, whose suicide rate rose almost 13 percent," the *Post* added. "Even more significant was a 32.3 percent spike in the number of suicides by suffocation, which is how Williams died."

Lahrs Mehlum, the director of Norway's Centre for Suicide Research and Prevention, told the *Post* that "many journalists failed to mention the huge health problems Williams struggled with (both mentally and physically), but rather portrayed a glorified version of the event. This is not according to international guidelines for media reporting of suicide.

"Another breach of these guidelines was the explicit reporting of the suicide method. The problem of these ways of reporting a suicide in the case of a celebrity is, of course, the real danger of copycat suicides."

their options. The evidence suggests that suicide 'outbreaks' and 'clusters' are real phenomena; one death can set off others. There's a particularly strong effect from celebrity suicides."

Madelyn Gould, a professor of epidemiology in psychiatry at Columbia University, who has studied suicide contagion extensively, told the newspaper: "Suicide contagion is real, which is why I'm concerned about it."

Sunnybrook Hospital's Dr. Mark Sinyor, who has published extensively on matters such as suicide prevention, says that if "an identifiable person dies by suicide, and it's widely reported, you will almost invariably see more suicides. For example, after the suicide of Robin Williams in 2014, there was an 11 percent increase in suicides, which was almost two thousand more people in the United States. And that finding was replicated in Canada, and in Australia. I published a study [in 2021] showing a five percent increase after the suicides of Anthony Bourdain and Kate Spade [in 2018]."

Reasons Why

A recent example of prospective social contagion is *13 Reasons Why*, a Netflix series that premiered in 2017. Based on a novel of the same name, it focuses on seventeen-year-old Hannah Baker, who has killed herself.

"She leaves behind 13 sides of cassette tapes, on which she has narrated the wrongdoings of those around her," the *Guardian* said in a review. "Each side concerns the actions of one of her acquaintances; they are supposed to listen, then pass the tapes to the next person, in order to learn what they've done, and so that it never has to happen again. Hannah is a martyr of teen angst. We see her tragedy unfold over two timelines, with flashbacks of how it all came to be, and a present-day story in which Clay (supposedly the nerdy, Star Wars–loving kid, with a jaw carved out of stone) attempts to unravel and then avenge the mystery."

In addition to suicide, the program explores issues such as bullying, rape, and sexual assault. Some mental health professionals, including Mark Sinyor, were extremely concerned about the potential influence it could have on suicide rates. "There was a huge outcry amongst the mental health community [when it was aired]," he says.

Sinyor wants to make it clear he's not against topics such as suicide being openly discussed. "The series producers ostensibly said that they wanted to start a conversation about mental illness and mental health. And, obviously, having a conversation about [these] is a good thing. I think the issue is that not all conversations are equal, in terms of their helpfulness and their value. What the show ends up doing is it sort of gives people a pathway to suicide. It explains why suicide happens. It suggests that it might be a helpful or useful strategy for coping with the kinds of difficulties young people face, and one of the unfortunate parts about it is that Hannah reaches out for support, and it doesn't work. Her school counsellor is not helpful to her, and so, the other message of the show is that reaching out is useless."

When the series premiered, the final episode depicted Hannah ending her life. The mental health community was so upset by this graphic scene that "Netflix did something they've never done — they actually deleted it [two years later]," Sinyor says.

Following the program's initial release, two studies examined the effects it might have had on suicide rates. "One was done by an international group, of which I was an author. And the other study was conducted by an American group," Sinyor says. His study looked at statistics involving young people between the ages of ten and nineteen; the other examined ages ten to seventeen. Although the results were slightly different, "the overarching collective finding was that there was an increase in suicides of more than ten percent in young people in the few months after the show came out. Our study suggested about a hundred or more teenagers, or young people [took their lives]."

Sinyor acknowledges that researchers can't say for certain that the Netflix series caused the suicide rates to increase. "It was just an association. But a group of us replicated the study in Ontario, and we found a similar increase in suicides here."

Another study "found there were more emergency department visits for self-harm in young people in Ontario after the show came out [but] not necessarily more visits to outpatient psychiatrists," he says. "If the show was helping [to] make things better, what you would hope, actually, is that young people might see their school counsellors, psychiatrists, or outpatient care, and so on. But instead, what we just found is people showing up to the emergency room after they had self-harmed."

The Papageno Effect

The second theory Sakinofsky described to the inquest is known as the Papageno effect.

In Mozart's most famous opera, *The Magic Flute*, which premiered in 1791, a bird catcher called Papageno contemplates suicide after losing the beautiful Papagena, whom he loves. Three spirits intervene and convince him there are other ways to deal with his pain and find happiness. He accepts their advice and is reunited with Papagena; together, they plan a family — a classic happy ending.

In 2010, Thomas Niederkrotenthaler, an associate professor and head of the Suicide Research & Mental Health Promotion unit at the Medical University of Vienna, along with seven others, published a paper entitled "Role of Media Reports in Completed and Prevented Suicide: Werther v. Papageno Effects." They aimed "to test the hypotheses that certain media content is associated with an increase in suicide, suggesting a so-called Werther effect, and that other content is associated with a decrease in suicide, conceptualized as a Papageno effect."

In dense academic language, the authors reported that, "repetitive reporting of the same suicide and the reporting of suicide myths were positively associated with suicide rates. Coverage of individual suicidal ideation not accompanied by suicidal behaviour was negatively associated with suicide rates." They concluded that "the impact of suicide reporting may not be restricted to harmful effects; rather, coverage of positive coping in adverse circumstances, as covered in media items about suicidal ideation, may have protective effects."

The U.S. National Suicide Prevention Lifeline summed up their findings in easier-to-follow wording: "Research shows that when details of positive coping during moments of crisis are included in media covering suicides, it may have a protective quality for those who may be experiencing thoughts of suicide themselves. On the other hand, continuous reporting of the same suicide and the reporting of suicide myths were associated with an increase in suicide rates (the Werther effect)."

In other words, if suicides are reported in a way that does not glamourize the act or give undue attention to the person who died in this manner, it might prevent a vulnerable individual from copying what they did. This appears to be especially true if the coverage includes positive information (such as solutions that don't involve suicide) and information about support services (such as a helpline).

Many people attempt to take their own lives on impulse, Sakinofsky told the inquest. "[They] forget the reasons for living in the heat of a crisis," he said.

But if somebody can reach out, offer a friendly hand, and help get a suicidal person over the critical impulsive period, lives can be saved, Sakinofsky said.

"WHY ARE YOU TAKING AWAY MY BRIDGE?"

Each time the suicide barrier successfully survived another veto at city hall, Birney and McCamus would receive strange or hateful phone calls.

One evening in mid-1998, a woman called Birney at his home from a blocked number and said, "Why are you taking away my bridge? I need that bridge." She explained that the Bloor Viaduct was her insurance policy.

The woman, who sounded as if she was middle-aged, said every day was a struggle for her. She saw the viaduct as a kind of escape hatch; and it comforted her to know it would be there if she needed to end her pain. "I was sexually abused as a child," she told Birney, "and I want to die where Martin Kruze died."

Birney kept her on the line as long as he could to try to get some identifying information: her name, place of employment, her doctor. She gave none. After she hung up, Birney called 911. The operator said that without a name, address, or phone number there was nothing they could do.

Whether or not the inquest jury agreed with him would soon become apparent. Its recommendations would be revealed in mid-July. "It wasn't a long time to wait," says Michael McCamus, "but Al and I nervously antici-pated what they would say."

Although city council had just approved a $1.5 million budget for a barrier design, by this point the two advocates had come to understand that politics could delay or derail a project unexpectedly. "We'd been told that it wasn't a *fait accompli* until a barrier was actually erected," says McCamus. "If the jury came out in strong support of, say, a suicide barrier, it might help ensure the success of our campaign."

Success can be a fickle mistress, however. "In the space of one week, these were two major victories for the barrier campaign that made Al and I feel that we were on top of the world, and the barrier was undeniable and unstoppable," McCamus says. "What we didn't know at that time was that unanimous votes of City Council and jury recommendations from a coroner's inquest could be ignored or overturned by future events. It was another important lesson in our education about local politics."

FEWER DEATHS IN VIENNA

In August 2001, the *Star*'s ombudsman, Robin Harvey, wrote a column on the editorial page. The headline was "Avoiding Copycats with Sensitivity." The article extolled the dramatic findings of a groundbreaking study demonstrat-ing that media coverage can increase the number of suicides.

She was referring to "Reporting on Suicides: Recommendations for the Media," a study authored by the American Foundation for Suicide Prevention; the American Association of Suicidology; and the Annenberg Public Policy Center, which is based at the University of Pennsylvania.

Under the heading, "Suicide Contagion Is Real," the study highlighted the work of journalists in Vienna who, between 1984 and 1987, covered the deaths of individuals who jumped in front of trains in the subway system.

"The coverage was extensive and dramatic," Harvey wrote. "In 1987, a campaign alerted reporters to the possible negative effects of such reporting and suggested alternate strategies for coverage.

"In the first six months after the campaign began, subway suicides and non-fatal attempts dropped by more than eighty percent. The total number of suicides in Vienna declined as well."

The research revealed there was an increase in suicides by readers or viewers when

- the number of stories about individual suicides increased;
- a particular death was reported at length or in many stories;
- the story of an individual death by suicide was placed on the front page or at the beginning of a broadcast; and
- the headlines about specific suicide deaths were dramatic (A recent example: "Boy, 10, Kills Himself Over Poor Grades").

While the study acknowledged that some suicides are newsworthy and have to be covered, "they also have the potential to do harm." It urged news organizations "to provide stories that inform readers and viewers about the causes of suicide, trends in suicide rates and recent treatment advances."

Harvey found the report's recommendations persuasive. She wrote that "news organizations should avoid any portrayal of suicide that may be viewed as heroic or romantic. They should not give detailed descriptions of suicide methods or detailed descriptions or pictures of the location of a suicide.

"They should not present suicide as an 'inexplicable act' of an otherwise healthy or high-achieving person. The report also says, whenever possible, to avoid referring to suicide in a headline."

Harvey also noted that, "When covering suicides, reporters should ask if the victim had received treatment for depression or any other mental health disorder and if he or she had a problem with substance abuse. This helps shed light on the varied and complex issues that may cause suicide."

Her final words: "All journalists would be wise to take the recommendations seriously."

9

The Media and Suicide

Although the majority of the mental health community accepts the validity of the Werther effect, there are dissenters.

One of the more prominent is André Picard, a highly respected reporter for the *Globe and Mail*, who specializes in health care issues. "[Proponents] cite this Austrian article in which a suicide was covered heavily and was followed by a rash of suicides — although I don't think that was proof of copycats. They are people that were on that path before, and I really don't think you can draw a conclusion one way or the other on that one," he wrote in 2009.

Thirteen years later, he reiterates that he has "mixed feelings" about the Werther effect. "I think a lot of those studies are done by people who are looking for a specific effect, and [so] you find it. I think there is some possibility of contagion, but I'm not sure the media is as powerful as people think it is," he says. "I don't think people read in the *Globe* that somebody jumped in front of a train at the Bloor station [subway stop in Toronto] and then say, 'Oh, I should go to the Bloor station and jump in front of a train.' I think it's a little more complicated than that."

When Canadian Press reporter Liam Casey was the editor of Toronto Metropolitan (formerly Ryerson) University's *Review of Journalism* in 2010, he also questioned the validity of the Werther effect. He had attempted suicide five years earlier and had strong, personal feelings about the subject. "Picard aside, few journalists have pushed the psychiatric community on the validity of the contagion effect," he wrote in an article entitled "Suicide Notes." "It's like a relic bomb from the Second World War that no one wants to examine, even though it's likely a dud. Stay away. Do not touch. Avoid."

Casey, who advocates openness when dealing with suicide, cites the case of Nadia Kajouji, an eighteen-year-old Carleton University student who ended her life in 2008 at the prompting of William Melchert-Dinkel, a former nurse from Minnesota. Melchert-Dinkel later confessed to advising the teen to kill herself while he was posing as a woman; he was convicted of attempting to assist in her suicide, as well as assisting in the suicide of another person.

"Kajouji's doctor and counsellor documented her distress: she walked her residence halls clutching razor blades, and an ambulance picked her up at a restaurant when she threatened to harm herself — a 2007 incident reported after her suicide and connection to Melchert-Dinkel came to light," Casey wrote. "The intense newspaper coverage, including in the *Toronto Star* and Sun Media, was like a torrential rainfall in an otherwise dry desert. 'Yes, I'd like to see the topic of suicide discussed more openly,' her brother says. 'If the Canadian public knew the severity of the issue, they'd respond well.'"

Despite Kajouji's brother's comments, Casey reported that Rajiv Bhatla, chief psychiatrist with the Royal Ottawa Health Care Group, criticized some of the media coverage. "'Excessive and detailed reporting of someone who commits suicide puts those contemplating suicide at risk and may also contribute to copycat suicides,'" he said. Curiously, he goes on to say that 'in order to prevent suicide we must be able to recognize it, talk about it, and treat it,'" Casey noted.

Whether to suppress or temper the reporting of suicide was a vexing question that André Picard explored in a September 2009 column about a University of Ottawa student who killed himself. Picard began by writing "how to cover suicides is one of the most difficult ethical dilemmas for journalists and editors." He cited the 3,473 suicides completed in Canada in 2005, the most recent year for which statistics were available at the time (Statistics Canada reported in 2023 that each year the number is approximately 4,500).

"What a tragic waste of life," he wrote. "Should we be turning a blind eye to this carnage so as to not offend sensibilities? Or should we be shining a light on suicide deaths — most of them preventable — to highlight the underlying cause, which is often untreated mental illness?"

Whether the media chooses to cover a suicide, as well as how they approach the topic, is governed by a mixed bag of guiding principles and practices, with no uniform code existing in Canada (the internet would make one impossible to enforce). In general, a suicide is only reported by the mainstream media if it involves a public person or has some relevance to the public. Obviously, that's quite subjective. As Picard rightly has pointed out, if the prime minister died by suicide, every detail would be reported and examined throughout the media. No media outlet of any stature would omit the prime minister's name, method of suicide, or where it took place.

A blanket policy would be unenforceable. What did emerge in the 1990s and afterward, however, was greater awareness of the potential effect that media coverage could have on people dealing with mental health matters. Positive changes lay ahead.

The Jury Speaks

In mid-1998, as Birney and McCamus awaited the findings of the Kenneth Au Yeung inquest, they, too, discussed the question of how to report suicides and whether Dr. Sakinofsky's proposals for the media were the right approach to adopt. "Al was passionate about this subject and sided with Sakinofsky," McCamus says. "As a journalism student at the time, I wondered if what he had proposed was reasonable. And more importantly, would the media agree to it?"

On July 10, 1998, the coroner's jury submitted its findings to the Ministry of the Solicitor General. It was apparent from the number of recommendations — twenty-three — and the scope of matters they touched upon that the five-member panel had not only paid close attention during the inquest, but had also given great care to what they believed needed to change as a result of Au Yeung's death.

Its third recommendation, addressed to the Ministry of Education, tackled the school's refusal to allow the young man to call his parents before being questioned: "The Ministry should publish [a student's right] to contact and have access to their parents in serious matters or in a behavioral crisis."

That rule already existed, McCamus says. "St. Mike's staff ignored it."

Recommendation number four, directed at the Toronto Police Service, dealt with Constable Downer's controversial role in what transpired: "If an off-duty officer is asked to be involved by [a] school for a non-emergent [*sic*] or non-criminal matter, the matter should be cleared with the appropriate supervisor and the events documented."

The tenth recommendation called for St. Michael's Choir School to "establish a committee to examine the culture and atmosphere of the school." This committee, it said, should include parents, students, teachers, principals and, possibly, school board psychologists.

Recommendation twenty-one, addressed to the City of Toronto, was particularly welcomed by Birney and McCamus: "[Council] is encouraged to approve and adopt the recommendations of the Urban Environment and Development Committee to establish measures directed toward deterrence of suicide attempts at the Prince Edward Viaduct."

They also celebrated number twenty-two, which dealt with the media. It showed that Dr. Sakinofsky's presentation had been convincing: "We recommend that every effort should be made to keep the location and method of suicide out of the media. If that is not possible, a low profile should be given to these matters."

While it was great to have such a thorough response to the decisions made and actions taken during Au Yeung's devastating situation, whether any would be enacted was another matter. What happened to the main protagonists following the inquest did not bode well for those who hoped for change and accountability.

Later that summer, the Toronto Catholic District School Board ruled that no disciplinary action would be taken against principal John Ryall. Board chair John Martino said that "Mr. Ryall's actions prior to, and following, Kenneth Au Yeung's death were consistent with board policy." Likewise, no censure was taken against French teacher Louise Kane, who had suggested to call Downer into the school that day. She was later promoted to guidance counsellor.

As for Constable Downer, it was revealed during the inquest that the police Professional Standards Review Committee had recommended disciplinary action be meted out, but police chief David Boothby vetoed its decision. Deputy chief Michael Boyd, who agreed with Boothby's ruling, testified at the inquest on June 30 that he believed Downer was just following community policing principles. It didn't matter that the constable was off duty and in another policing jurisdiction when he questioned the students. Downer was later promoted to the rank of detective.

THE JURY GETS ITS WISHES

On September 9, 1999, deputy coroner Dr. Bonita Porter announced that twenty-one of the jury's recommendations had or would be implemented.

They included a new suicide prevention education program at the Toronto Catholic District School Board.

10

The TTC Pushes the Stop Button

B irney and McCamus didn't have much time to celebrate the Kenneth Au Yeung jury's recommendations before another potential problem emerged. On July 22, the Toronto Transit Commission (TTC), in what it believed was a response to the Request for Proposals for barrier designs, informed the Works department that it used a truck-mounted crane, known as the Bridgemaster, to inspect the viaduct's subway deck.

In retrospect, the TTC should have been invited onto the Bloor Viaduct Project Steering Committee (PSC) at the onset, says Les Kelman. "If we had … I'm not sure it would have sparked their negative reaction [later on]." The TTC said it needed to have input into the barrier design to ensure the crane could continue to perform its function.

Its intervention came too late. The competition was already underway. Accommodating the TTC's inspections was not included in the design requirements.

"I didn't buy their argument," says Howard Moscoe, TTC chair at the time. "The Veil could have been constructed in a way that would not, in any way, have interfered with the TTC's access to the tracks."

Why, then, did the TTC raise such a fuss? "Because they're an innately conservative organization," he says. "And they're very difficult to deal with. They over-engineer everything, and they're super cautious about safety. I once asked a developer [who worked with them] at the end of a process:

'How would you describe your working relationship with the TTC?' And he said, 'I'd rather have pins pushed into my eyeballs.'"

Although the TTC had lost this initial skirmish, Birney, McCamus, and the other members of the Project Steering Committee knew the victory could be short-lived. The TTC was a powerful force in the city. "We doubted it would just walk away and not mount a counter-offensive," McCamus says.

How true that turned out to be.

In October 1998, the Works department summoned the Project Steering Committee to Metro Hall where the TTC, once again, contended that the five-metre Veil would obstruct the Bridgemaster crane and prevent the TTC from inspecting the subway track. Although this was not the only way the track could be inspected, it was the one the TTC preferred.

As the Bridgemaster moved slowly along the viaduct's upper roadway, the TTC said, inspectors could peer up at the subway's supports to look for signs of damage, age, or weathering. The difficulty was that the Veil, at five metres high, would obstruct the crane and make the Bridgemaster obsolete. But TTC's annual inspections of the lower deck were indispensable to the proper maintenance and safety of the subway tracks.

Kelman explained to the PSC members that the Works department and TTC staff were trying to find alternative ways to continue the safety inspections, including one that would surprise everyone. That turned out to be an understatement.

At the meeting Tom Denes of the Works department said they had asked Dereck Revington if he could modify the design of the Luminous Veil so it could be "removed" once a year to accommodate the Bridgemaster.

Birney and McCamus were dumbfounded.

"People will jump when the barrier is down," Birney whispered to McCamus.

"Of all the bridges we've studied, none had a removable barrier," McCamus told Denes.

"Yes," Denes replied matter-of-factly, "but none of them had a subway train either."

Despite Moscoe's assertion that there wasn't really a problem, the TTC and the Works department became embroiled in a protracted, bureaucratic tug-of-war over the design and cost of the Luminous Veil. The latter wanted to proceed with the barrier; senior TTC staff had strong reservations about safety and design issues and, especially, the cost. Consequently, construction of the barrier was delayed.

To Birney's frustration, the PSC did not meet again until spring 1999.

"The TTC staff took a completely legitimate safety concern and turned it into a totally unnecessary, five-month filibuster during which three more people died at the bridge," says Michael McCamus. "It didn't need to be that way."

In February 1999, Works staff informed Birney and McCamus that the barrier project continued to be held up. They were told that the TTC and

A SCOLDING

At the end of the October 1998 Bloor Viaduct Project Steering Committee meeting, Les Kelman told McCamus he was upset with a letter the young man had published in the *Star* a few days earlier.

In the letter, "Many to Thank for Bloor Viaduct Safety Screen," McCamus said councillors Pam McConnell and Jack Layton had been "drafted as foot soldiers but were not the generals leading the charge" for the suicide barrier.

He mildly criticized them for getting the credit, and then named everyone on the steering committee and their contribution: Birney, Superintendent Maher, orthopaedic surgeon Dr. Robin Richards, Karen Letofsky, Dr. Isaac Sakinofsky, Dr. Paul Links, and Ray and Mary Doucette.

"I couldn't believe it," Kelman said. "Before you write a letter like that, maybe you should consider whether or not you still want the councillors' support," which the steering committee needed to solve the mess with the Toronto Transit Commission.

He confronted McCamus at what turned out to be Kelman's last steering committee meeting. He was replaced by Tom Denes, a seasoned civil servant from the old city of Etobicoke, before amalgamation.

the Works department had still failed to agree on an alternative inspection method for the viaduct's subway level, although there were five other possible solutions. To Birney, the delay was totally unacceptable.

Birney's annoyance would only escalate in mid-March when the Works department released a report saying the estimated cost of the Luminous Veil had ballooned to $2.5 million, one million more than the approved budget. Works recommended the Luminous Veil be cancelled; the so-called "runner-up" design from E.R.A. Architects of the 1998 design contest be substituted; the City install emergency crisis phones on the viaduct; and the Schizophrenia Society establish foot patrols on the viaduct.

"We were stunned," says McCamus. "There was no 'runner-up' design. Only the Veil met all the requirements. It was virtually the unanimous choice."

Joe Pantalone Saves the Day

On March 23, after having held meetings and hearing deputations from Birney, McCamus, and Superintendent Maher, the TTC issued a report it surely knew would roil the waters at city hall: it needed council to approve $800,000 to purchase a new, taller Bridgemaster crane.

IN HOWARD'S WORDS

Few city councillors were as colourful or outspoken as Howard Moscoe. "He is a giant of a man, probably six foot four or taller and looks like Fred Flintstone or [the actor] John Goodman," says McCamus. "He liked to crack jokes when reporters and cameras were around, such as comparing the Veil to a giant egg slicer. That kind of remark was typical of his sense of humour."

Moscoe began his work life as a junior high school art teacher with the North York Board of Education. He was also a successful businessman, having designed and produced plastic sleeves to prevent damage from rainwater for election signs.

He entered politics in 1978, winning a seat on the North York City Council. When he retired in 2010, at age seventy, he had spent thirty-two years in Toronto politics.

Over the years, he was particularly fond of taking jibes at Mayor Lastman. "In a city where the native tongue of many councillors is Politically Correct, Moscoe was often good for an unabashed take on all things Toronto," the *Toronto Star* said upon his retirement. "'A calypso dancer couldn't crawl under my opinion of Mel Lastman,' he said in 2003 of the former mayor."

Asked why he disliked Lastman so much — both were Jewish politicians with working-class roots — he says today that "Mel represented the stereotype I've been trying to live down all my life — a fast-talking hustler. You've heard of love-hate relationships. This is a hate-hate relationship."

One time, Lastman donated one of his toupées at a charity auction. "My wife bought it for thirty-five bucks," Moscoe says. "I used to drive him nuts, 'cause I'd come into a council meeting, open my briefcase, take out his toupée, and use it to dust off my chair and the desk around it. At one time, I felt sorry for him, because he used to come to council meetings on Mondays with terrible headaches. Until I learned they were hair aches, and that he was having plugs transplanted in his head. That's when I lost all sympathy."

Moscoe says he still has the toupée and has been offered up to a thousand dollars for it.

Another story involves Councillor Betty Disero, who was making a plea for streetcar service in her ward when Moscoe was chair of the Toronto Transit Commission. When she finished her presentation, he said: "One question: Will it be a streetcar named Disero?"

During the suicide-barrier campaign, Moscoe was one of its strongest supporters. When he had first met Birney and McCamus in March 1998, he said, "I think it's well known that if you go back far enough, everyone has mental illness in their family."

Councillor Joe Pantalone, chair of the UED committee, came to the rescue. He chaired two meetings on the matter, on March 31 and April 19, 1999. At the first one, the UED committee adopted the Works' recommendations for emergency crisis phones and foot patrols (an idea that was never enacted) but deferred the barrier-and-crane-cost issue to a meeting on April 19.

In preparation for what was the fifth UED committee meeting to consider the barrier issue, Birney and McCamus arranged for letters to be presented from suicide researchers around the world, including Montreal; Washington, D.C.; New Jersey; Chicago; Oakland; Texas A&M University; Bristol, England; and Brisbane, Australia. Letters also came from Ben Au Yeung and former finance minister Wilson.

Led by chair Joe Pantalone, a member of the NDP, the UED committee voted to approve $800,000 for a new Bridgemaster crane and an additional $1 million for the Luminous Veil suicide barrier.

"Joe rejected the proposal to award the contract to E.R.A., the so-called runner-up design. He saved the project," says McCamus. "Revington was not fired. We felt a great deal of relief."

Everything was set, but the project would now have to pass muster with the powerful budget chief, Tom Jakobek.

"WE DON'T EAT IN PLACES LIKE THAT"

In the late nineties, Al Birney often spoke at Schizophrenia Society of Ontario events about mental health issues.

As a thank you for one of his presentations, he was given a gift certificate to Mizzen, the upscale restaurant in Toronto's Westin Harbour Castle hotel.

"I'm not sure what to do with it," he said to McCamus. "Kathleen and I don't eat in places like that."

His solution was to invite Michael's parents, Ruth and Walter, to join them. "Neither of our families could afford to eat an expensive meal in such a palatial place," Michael says. "It was a nice way for the families to bond."

11

Death on the Rails

The Toronto Transit Commission (TTC) was on the minds of Al Birney and Michael McCamus in 1999, not only because of the transit system's attempted filibuster of the viaduct barrier. They also considered the subway system to be another suicide magnet, as great a concern as the viaduct, if not more. "We were as passionate about the need for some form of suicide prevention on the TTC," says McCamus, "but we simply didn't have the time or energy to take that on."

If they had found some politicians, bureaucrats, and journalists resistant to a barrier on the viaduct, that opposition paled compared to the unwillingness of the TTC to consider even discussing the subject.

The TTC's intransigence was soon going to be confronted, partly triggered by several highly publicized "incidents," as the TTC referred to suicide attempts and suicide deaths, and a media campaign aimed at reversing its policy.

The first took place in the early evening of Sunday, August 22. Jeyabalan Balasingam left his Scarborough, Ontario, home with his three-year-old son, Sajanthan. The forty-one-year-old told his wife, Uma, who was taking care of their yet-to-be-named nineteen-day-old daughter, that he was going to visit a friend.

Balasingam, who had been struggling with depression and feelings of paranoia for several years, instead took his son to the Victoria Park subway station, where they stood on the westbound platform waiting for a train. As one approached, Balasingam grabbed Sajanthan, stepped off the platform and dropped onto the track below. Their bodies were found underneath the second-last car. Both were dead.

Two days later, the *Toronto Star* quoted his psychiatrist as saying Balasingam had been taking his medications inconsistently since the previous winter. It also reported that his mental health had worsened after the birth of his daughter.

The newspaper felt it necessary to explain that "it does not normally report suicides but is covering the incident because it was also a murder."

Three months later, thirty-five-year-old Uma spoke with *Star* reporter Michelle Shephard about her life with Balasingam, whom she had wed in an arranged marriage in her native country of Sri Lanka, in 1993. Soon after their marriage, she moved to Canada with her husband, who had already been living there for about four years.

At first, all was well, but by 1995, "Balasingam began beating his wife, and the paranoia and depression started. He drank heavily," Shephard reported.

"When people with mental illness try to use drugs or alcohol to cope with their symptoms of mental illness, it's sometimes referred to as 'self-medicating,'" says McCamus. "It's why there's a huge overlap of mental health and addiction problems."

Zarina Sherazee, a family counsellor with South Asian Family Support Services, told the newspaper that seeking treatment for mental health problems was rare among her Sri Lankan clients: "Back in their country, there's a stigma attached to seeking help and if you go to a psychiatrist, you're considered to be 'stark raving mad.'"

This was one of the key points former finance minister Michael Wilson had been trying to communicate in his speeches — that the stigma often makes people in many communities, if not most, feel ashamed of their illness and unwilling to ask for help.

The front-page stories about the tragedy brought three issues involving the TTC and suicide to light: whether the TTC should install safety barriers to prevent people from jumping in front of trains; the psychological effects train drivers often experience after witnessing a death on the tracks; and whether the TTC should publicly report statistics about suicide fatalities and attempts.

The third issue was of particular concern to some members of the media, who believed the TTC's unwillingness to share this information deeply impacted the other two.

The Silent Treatment

For most of its history, the TTC had a policy of not releasing information or statistics to the media and the public on subway suicides for fear of copycat incidents. The *Globe*'s André Picard disagreed with that approach and, possibly, the TTC's motivation. "I think they should be much more transparent," he says. "Maybe because I'm a journalist, but I just believe that that information should be out there. I don't think we have to report it in, you know, a scurrilous way, or a way that's inflammatory, but I think that data should be out there. I don't think hiding it benefits anyone. I've often wondered if the reluctance is because of the cost of suicide barriers, such as [the ones] they have in other countries, like Japan."

The policy likely originated in the early 1970s, when two Toronto coroners' inquests into subway suicides recommended "gates" be built in the TTC subway system. In 1971, the TTC issued statements saying gates would be too expensive, they might not be safe during operation, and may not even be mechanically possible to implement.

Concerned about the possible contagion effect of reporting subway suicides in the media — at that time, jumpers were identified, and a coroner's inquest was held — the coroner's office asked in the early 1970s if the media would voluntarily agree not to print any stories about subway suicides, as an experiment for six months, to see if suicides would decrease. The media complied, unless the person was a public figure or there was a perceived need for the public to know the details. As a result, the voluntary ban continued for many decades to come. At the same time, the TTC stopped talking to the media about suicide statistics, a policy that remained in effect in the mid-2000s, when another widely covered suicide occurred.

On Friday morning, August 11, 2000, the TTC's reluctance to say anything seemed like the classic ostrich-in-the-sand approach when Dr. Suzanne Killinger-Johnson, a thirty-seven-year-old Toronto psychotherapist, jumped in front of a train as she clutched her sleeping six-month-old son. He died immediately; she remained in hospital for nine days before succumbing to her injuries.

"There is an unwritten policy not to talk about suicides, and not to encourage them," TTC board chair Howard Moscoe said, when asked to comment on the incident. It sounded heartless and obfuscatory. "It seemed to me and Al that the TTC should have said, 'Never again. Come hell or high water, we will stop this,'" McCamus remembers. "To our disappointment and many people's shock, that didn't happen."

The story gripped Toronto for several news cycles, especially after it was revealed that police had twice escorted Killinger-Johnson away from other subway platforms the day before she jumped. Following her second attempt, police drove her home.

Interest continued to rise when it was learned that both her parents were doctors and well informed about stress, depression, and anxiety. The *Globe* noted that "her father, Donald Killinger, was a specialist in internal medicine and endocrinology in London, Ontario. Her mother, Barbara Killinger, was a Toronto psychologist and author who has written about dealing with anxiety and depression."

Following the death of Killinger-Johnson, Karen Letofsky said during a meeting of the Bloor Viaduct Project Steering Committee (PSC) that she and Dr. Links had started discussions with the TTC on how it could reduce suicides in the subway. Even if barriers were off the table, what other methods could be used?

Around this time, the TTC started a program called "Gatekeepers," in which TTC subway staff were trained to look for suspicious behaviour and warning signs of people about to jump, such as lingering on the platform too long or pacing back and forth. It was a simple but effective initiative. TTC spokesperson Brad Ross would later point out that the number of incidents in the following years decreased. "It's literally saving lives," he said.

Almost a decade after Killinger-Johnson's suicide, a high-profile pushing incident that involved three teenage boys, one of whom was the son of the *Globe and Mail*'s then editor-in-chief Eddie Greenspon, became headline news.

About 4:30 p.m. on Friday, February 13, 2009, Eddie's son, Jacob, stood on a subway platform with two friends. They were on their way to Jacob's house to celebrate his fifteenth birthday. As an eastbound train approached, Adenir De Oliveira, a forty-nine-year-old Portuguese immigrant, stood nearby on the platform. The *Globe* later reported that De Oliveira looked "remarkably like the perfect department store Santa Claus, white-bearded, chubby cheeks, utterly benign." De Oliveira pushed Jacob and one of the other boys, fourteen-year-old Asaf Shargall, into the path of the train. He failed in his attempt to do the same to the third boy.

There was no known provocation for the assault.

The Silence Ends

About eighteen months after the subway pushing incident, TTC subway operator Jack Gajic testified at De Oliveira's trial on three charges of attempted murder and two counts of assault. He said that on the day of the incident he saw "what looked like kids horsing around on the platform ahead as his train thundered through the tunnel toward Dufferin station."

Suddenly, he said, two of the boys closest to the edge toppled onto the tracks, the *Star* reported. Gajic hit the emergency brakes. "One boy rolled underneath the platform, the second (boy) seemed frozen. He was looking right at me," Gajic said.

"Gajic, a 9½-year TTC veteran, described seeing a pair of hands reach out from underneath the platform and felt 'two bumps' before the train screeched to a halt. 'I thought I killed him or at the very least cut his legs off,'" he told the *Star*.

Jacob was likely saved from death when Asaf pulled him to safety. But the train struck his left leg and he subsequently lost several toes. Asaf, who was later awarded a Governor General's Star of Courage for his actions under extreme duress, suffered minor injuries.

In late October 2010, De Oliveira was found not criminally responsible on all counts, based on testimony about his mental health over the years.

Later that year, on Saturday, October 3, David Dewees, a thirty-two-year-old Toronto high school teacher, chose the subway to end his life. The previous Thursday, Dewees had been charged with sex exploitation after he was alleged to have inappropriately contacted two male teens he had met while volunteering at Pioneer Camp Ontario, a Christian fellowship camp near Huntsville, Ontario. It was assumed he had taken his life because of "the weight of guilt or the heavy prospect of proving his innocence," the *Toronto Star* reported.

Despite these highly publicized incidents, the TTC's silent treatment continued until November 2009, when the Ontario Information and Privacy Commissioner (IPC) ruled that it must release some of the contentious statistics.

James Wallace, the *Toronto Sun*'s editor-in-chief, said publicly that subway operators had contacted his reporters to tell them about the distress they were experiencing over suicides they had witnessed. He told *Toronto Life* magazine, "From our perspective, there were a number of legitimate public policy issues at stake. The only way for us to know the extent of the problem was to get statistical evidence. For all we knew, the death toll was outrageous." The TTC refused to give the *Sun* numbers. Wallace called the commission's attitude "obstructionist," and the paper made a successful appeal to Ontario's Information and Privacy Commissioner.

As a TTC announcement issued on November 26, 2009, made clear, the transit authority reluctantly complied:

"The Toronto Transit Commission has been ordered to release subway suicide statistics from 1998 to 2007 under the Municipal Freedom of Information and Protection of Privacy Act. A local media outlet made a request to the TTC one year ago for statistics related to the number of people who take their lives annually on the subway. The TTC denied that request citing health and safety concerns, and the contagion, or copycat, effect suicide reporting may pose, particularly as it relates to the method of suicide. On appeal, the IPC ordered the statistics released."

As a result of the compliance order, it was revealed that from 1987 to 2007, 150 people had died from being hit by a train, about one person per month. The *Sun* soon after reported that since the subway opened in 1954, there had been more than 1,200 incidents on the TTC.

No matter whether the numbers were declining, as Brad Ross had said some years earlier, barrier advocates believed the TTC needed to follow the lead of cities such as Tokyo, Paris, Dubai, and Shanghai, and install safety doors that would prevent passenger access to a track until a train had stopped.

The news the PSC longed to hear came in late March 2010 when the TTC board of commissioners agreed to include funding for platform screen doors in its 2011–2015 capital budget. "Suicide prevention doors could be arriving at the [main] Yonge St. subway line early as 2013," the *Toronto Sun* reported. "But TTC officials acknowledge it will take untold years and up to $690 million to bring the life-saving devices to the entire subway system."

The newspaper added that the decision came "under pressure to deal with the tragic death toll on its tracks. Outfitting a single station with PSDs [platform screen doors] could cost up to $10 million, while requiring the installation of automatic controls and new trains. But the cost of not taking action, the commission heard, was high."

Toronto lawyer Lindsay Hill, who had been diagnosed with a serious mental illness, told the board that some people might not be able to resist the opportunity to kill themselves, even though they really did want to live.

"Sometimes you walk down to the TTC platform and you hear silence and then you hear the rushing wind, and you think it would be so easy," she said. "And that calls to you and the decision is out of your hand."

Pediatrician Dr. Jeffrey Seidman, the *Sun* reported, said not all victims are deliberately committing suicide: "Some people have fallen or been pushed on to the tracks. Operators and witnesses are often traumatized by the events."

Driving Hazards

Many operators who were driving a train that killed or maimed a jumper indeed suffered an emotional toll from the harrowing experience. Few talked about it publicly, likely because of the TTC's adamant refusal up until 2009 to discuss the matter in public or to name a jumper.

The reluctance of drivers to share their reactions to having hit a jumper changed in May 2011 with the release of a nine-minute documentary, *Chance Encounters*, which featured interviews with Kevin and Shelley Pett, husband-and-wife TTC subway operators who both experienced driving over a suicidal person with their subway train.

Early on Saturday morning, October 3, 2009, Kevin saw a man acting strangely as he guided his train eastbound into High Park Station. "From the moment I saw him, my first thought was, *What is this guy doing? Like, is he playing chicken?*" he said in the documentary. "His ... his body was shaking uncontrollably. It was just going up and down, up and down, with his head on the running rail. I remember yelling at him, like, get up, get up, get up. When he looked at me, and our eyes met, time just stood still. It felt like driving a car over railroad tracks, that rumbling feeling that you get when you go over the tracks, that's how it felt. And I realized then that I had just killed somebody."

The man was David Dewees, the high school teacher facing sexual abuse charges. Because his death was widely reported, Kevin soon learned exactly who he'd hit.

Kevin had difficulty functioning after the incident, likely due to PTSD. "I didn't want to do anything. I wouldn't want to get up," he said.

His inability to function well upset Shelley. "I was angry at him for a while, only because I felt that, okay, it happened, but you need to function, and he couldn't."

Her attitude, and her understanding of what her husband was experiencing, changed two and a half months later when she, too, hit someone, a few feet short of the Broadview station. "This guy jumps out in front of me, and I didn't want to remember any of this, I didn't want to see it. I didn't want to hear it. And I tucked my feet up, and I covered my ears with my hand, and

I closed my eyes, and I screamed," she said in the documentary. "I just kept, remember saying to everybody, my husband just had the suicide, there's … this can't be happening, there's no way.

"Having to go to bed was probably the scariest thing I ever had to do. But I thought, *how do you do that*? How do you know that … you were a part of someone's death? How do you go to sleep? My house has never been so clean. I'd stay up till three or four o'clock in the morning, scrubbing my floors, just because I didn't want to sit down and think about what had happened."

In some cases, drivers and other TTC staff who witness incidents that don't result in a death suffer just as much emotional turmoil. In fact, "only 60% of people who jump die," *Toronto Life* reported in 2010. "Organs are destroyed, limbs are amputated or crushed, and hemorrhaging is extensive."

TTC operators have post-traumatic stress disorder at four times the rate of police officers, the *National Post* reported in June 2017. It also noted that "61% of the [people they hit] had underlying psychiatric illnesses such as depression, schizophrenia and psychosis."

Some years earlier, the *Toronto Sun* reported that "a Workplace Safety & Insurance Board funded study found that the TTC has the greatest number of traumatic psychological claims in Ontario. As one subway driver [said]: 'Everyone deals with [the mental toll] differently. Some drivers come back the next day, some drivers never come back to the subway or they transfer out." Some never come back to the TTC at all.

"We actually mandate people take time off if they're operating at the time of a suicide, or an attempt," TTC spokesperson Stuart Green said in 2023.

The Petts were among those who returned to their jobs, after some time spent trying to deal with what they'd each experienced. But it wasn't easy. "My first time driving into that station, I saw him jump in front of me again," Kevin said. Shelley had a similar reaction. "I remember going into Broadview [station] and closing my eyes. I just, I closed, and I kind of … because I could see him. I could see him jumping in front of me, all over again."

At the end of the short film, Kevin said that if he kept thinking about what had happened, he was "gonna go crazy. I had to put it out of my mind." It's still part of their lives, Shelley said. "We all deal with it. My family does, my husband does, every day."

A LIFE-SAVING LINK

In mid-June 2011, the Toronto Transit Commission (TTC) announced another suicide prevention initiative: phones throughout the subway system, as well as signs indicating their location, that were linked directly to a dedicated crisis line operated by Distress Centres of Greater Toronto. "It was the first of its kind in North America," says Karen Letofsky, the Distress Centres' executive director. "It's one-of-a-kind." Much of the phone infrastructure was paid for by Bell Canada.

Called Crisis Link, the hundred-thousand-dollar program was designed to prevent people from taking their lives, TTC spokesperson Brad Ross told the media.

"Despite multiple mitigation attempts ... the numbers show no sign of declining: Twenty-six people killed themselves in 2010, Mr. Ross said; [as of June 2011], seven people have committed suicide on Toronto's public transit," the *Globe* said.

A Gatekeeper to the Rescue

At the beginning of May 2017, John Paul Attard, a TTC collector, saw a man walk by him and then lower himself onto the tracks at Dundas Station, CBC News reported. Within seconds Attard had alerted transit control to cut power to the station.

"Amid all the bustle, he quietly sat down at the edge of the platform and looked into the man's eyes," CBC said. He asked the man: "Are you having a bad day?"

"Yes, I want to hurt myself," the man replied.

"That's when I just kind of embraced him and hugged him," Attard said.

For the next twenty minutes, the two talked, with Attard, who suffers from mental health concerns himself, "putting [positive] affirmations in his mind," their "conversation spanning hip-hop music to what the future held," the CBC said. "I will be your mentor, I will take care of you," Attard told the man.

Attard convinced the twenty-three-year-old to abandon his suicide attempt. "Here's a situation where someone approaches someone who was in distress, listens to the person, providing listening, providing the support and care, and it made all the difference," Dr. Katy Kamkar, a clinical psychologist at the Centre for Addiction and Mental Health, told the CBC.

Peer Support

The Gatekeeper program was replaced in 2018. That year, the TTC began a peer-to-peer support program for employees who needed to talk about problems they were dealing with on the job. "We're not counsellors, by any stretch. We don't replace any sort of clinical counselling, or professional counselling," says volunteer Jason Banfield, a streetcar operator for more than two decades.

"They deal more with the clinical end, but we deal with the street or rail end. How it could have played out, what it looked like, the reaction that the operator had, and what they did. It's more than, say, a layperson would understand.

"You tend to talk more openly around people you work with, because they get it. It's just nice to talk to someone who's in the trenches with you, someone who understands the subtle nuances, the lingo, and the way things work at the TTC."

Banfield never had to deal with a suicide as a driver, but his streetcar did hit and kill a woman in 2003. "I don't believe she intended on taking her life," he says. "She ran in front of me to catch the streetcar going in the other direction, and I made contact because it was a dark and dreary, rainy November day."

Banfield says he didn't realize how traumatic the experience had been until a couple of years later when "we started to have a rash of suicides on the subway. I started thinking about it again. It forced me to re-evaluate life and understand how precious it is and how short time can be — and it's part of the reason I'm involved with safety to this day."

He is able to share his post-accident reactions with fellow employees. They can ask for a peer who works in the same area as them, although it isn't a requirement.

For example, he's supported drivers who've dealt with a suicide on the subway, seeking advice from his father, who was a subway driver for more than thirty years and had been involved in three suicides.

"I think the biggest hurdle that these folks face is replaying the event over and over again in their head, in their sleep," he says. "When they're awake, and they can talk about other things, you know, their mind doesn't necessarily wander. But when they're on their own, or they're going to sleep, they replay the event."

He says "the vast majority of people are very appreciative, and the peer support program is very well received. We are really just there to be a sounding board. I call it water cooler conversation, but the kind that can sometimes involve pretty difficult topics."

Banfield says he really believes in this kind of program: "I think it could be applied to just about any occupation on Earth."

$1.5 Billion Price Tag

At the end of September 2022, the TTC completed its Automatic Train Control (ATC) signalling system on Line 1 (Yonge–University), its longest line at almost 38.8 kilometres, which serves thirty-eight stations. The new system replaced one that had been in place since the 1950s.

One of the main advantages of ATC is its ability to allow trains to safely run more closely together, which means improved service.

It also opens the doors, so to speak, for the eventual installation of platform edge doors that would prevent suicides, says TTC spokesperson Stuart Green. "Chiefly because of technical reasons, platform edge doors can only work when you have [ATC]. It's a system where computers drive the train, and they stop it at the exact same spot, like on a dime, every single time."

Platform edge doors (PEDs), also known as platform screen doors, physically separate rail tracks from platforms. Once installed, PEDs make it impossible for riders to access the trains until a subway car has entered a station and completely stopped. In recent years, they have become widely used in newer metro systems, especially in Europe and Asia.

All new TTC stations will have ATC, Green says, "and will be built to a spec that would allow them to easily accommodate PEDs. All the rest of our system would require massive overhauls, and that's why the cost … the price tag is so high."

As of 2022, that price tag was approximately $1.5 billion, says Green. (In 2014, when the estimate for PEDs was considerably less, the *Star*'s Rosie DiManno had this to say: "A billion dollars to install anti-suicide barriers in Toronto's 69 subway stations? Are you friggin' kidding me?")

In mid-April 2022, the controversial issue once again made the news.

On Easter Sunday, April 17, at about 9:00 p.m., thirty-nine-year-old Shamsa Al-Balushi was waiting for a train at the busy Bloor-Yonge station. A woman unknown to her pushed her onto the track.

Al-Balushi managed to crawl underneath the covered part of the platform and avoided being hit by the incoming train. She did, however, suffer serious injuries from the fall.

The day following the assault, police arrested forty-five-year-old Edith Frayne and charged her with attempted murder. It was later determined that she had "consumed an excessive amount of alcohol, medications and/ or illicit substances, and was impaired at the time," according to the TTC.

The following month, lawyers for the victim launched a one-million-dollar lawsuit against the TTC. They asserted that Al-Balushi incurred, and will continue to incur, medical expenses for medication, therapy, rehabilitation, and other forms of care, and that her ability to earn an income has been reduced. They also alleged that not enough was done by the TTC to prevent the attack, and that the company "failed to promptly respond to the incident."

The claim said "that while the assailant who pushed Al-Balushi onto the tracks was not employed by or affiliated with the TTC, the TTC is liable for the incident," *CBC News* reported.

A DUTY OF CARE?

In late April, *Toronto Star* columnist Heather Mallick weighed in on the barrier controversy (the following remarks have been edited).

"The TTC needs platform gates at every station that open onto each train door as the train arrives. Basic stuff. There will be fewer murders, not to mention suicides, accidents, and delays, and fewer train operators and passengers left devastated by what they saw and heard that day.

"Such barriers have been discussed for decades in cities across Canada. Tokyo has them, as does Copenhagen and Hong Kong. Why does Toronto have such a small puddle of ambition in its architecture, transit, and green transformation?

"Part of the problem, of course, was Premier Doug Ford cutting Toronto City Council by almost half, handing power to suburban wards that have different problems than urban ones. This spells death to progressive or sensible centrist ideas (but there is no intrinsic reason this should be so).

"So think of the consequences as you go about the city: no sliding doors, no attention to details. I imagine the woman under that platform. What duty of care did we owe her?"

"The TTC … failed to implement sufficient safety protocols on the subway platform; failed to provide regular supervision of the passengers; did not have adequate surveillance of the platform; failed to promptly respond to the incident, the claim says."

In June, *CityNews* reported that it had obtained a statement of defence by the TTC, which said it wasn't liable for what happened, especially because Al-Balushi "failed to take reasonable steps and precautions for her own safety and protection."

The TTC also said Al-Balushi "chose to stand close to the edge of the platform" and "failed to pay due care and attention to her surroundings." TTC lawyers also proposed that Al-Balushi "knew or was familiar with Edith

Frayne," and that she should have removed herself from the situation. They also said Al-Balushi shouldn't have been travelling on the subway alone, because "she knew or ought to have known that it was unsafe for her to do so."

CityNews put that allegation to Darryl Singer, a commercial and civil lawyer with the Toronto law firm Diamond & Diamond. "To go so far as to blame the victim for this is shocking and appalling and I can't believe they would actually commit that to writing in a court document," he said. "It's a public transit service. It's designed for people to move from place to place. So, if they really want to stick to that defence, then what they're really saying to the population of the GTA [Greater Toronto Area] is don't ride the subway because it's not safe."

JAPAN LEADS THE WAY

Beginning in the late 1990s, when Japan's suicide rate was at its peak, Japanese rail operators began a number of initiatives to curb incidences of suicide-by-train, the *Globe and Mail* reported in August 2017.

"Gliding into stations along Tokyo's flagship Yamanote Line, the bustling line connecting the capital's largest and busiest stations, one is greeted by a chest-high metal barrier whose doors open automatically upon a train's arrival. Known formally as Platform Screen Doors (PSDs), these barriers along a platform's edge are designed to prevent incursions — intentional or otherwise — onto the tracks.

"According to one 2015 study, installation of such PSDs in Tokyo rail and subway stations resulted in 76-per-cent fewer suicide attempts. Floor-to-ceiling barriers, as used in some Tokyo subway stations, as well as the metro systems in Hong Kong and Moscow, all but eliminate the possibility of track incursion."

Outfitting twenty-four of the twenty-nine stations of Tokyo's Yamanote Line with platform barriers cost roughly $11 million per station — a number in line with estimates for installing barriers in Toronto's subway stations.

12

Al Birney's Shining Moment

Howard Moscoe believed it wasn't necessary to continue to delay work on the barrier. On June 15, 1998, after the Urban Environment and Development (UED) committee had endorsed the $1.5 million budget for the Veil, the councillor had triumphantly told the *Toronto Star*, "The barriers are a go, unless something unforeseen happens."

The unforeseen did indeed happen, more than once, and the source of the latest snag was the powerful public transit authority whose senior staff were, ironically, accountable to Moscoe as its chair.

That the left-leaning Moscoe, a passionate supporter of public transit, was in charge of the Toronto Transit Commission (TTC) was, in itself, somewhat of a surprise. Six months earlier, when newly elected mayor Mel Lastman had selected Moscoe as his pick to lead the TTC, many political observers were surprised, given their history. During their time together on North York City Council, prior to amalgamation, Lastman and Moscoe had been combative — and sometimes comical — rivals.

Despite their enmity, in an interview with the *Toronto Star*, Lastman said he chose Moscoe because he believed he'd "do a good job." But he added a caveat: "The thing is, a councillor or a mayor cannot get in there and run the [TTC]. You've got to let the department heads run the department."

This comment was likely in response to bitter complaints from David Gunn, TTC chief general manager, who claimed Moscoe had frequently interfered in management decisions — such as Moscoe supporting the barrier without considering the TTC's concerns about accessing the viaduct for safety inspections — rather than sticking to his policy-making role.

Gunn had been hired at the start of 1995 by the old Metro Council. Eight months later, on August 11, a subway crash — one train rear-ended another in a tunnel between the St. Clair West and Dupont Stations — killed three people and injured thirty others. The TTC was seriously reeled by the deadliest accident in a rapid transit system in Canadian history. A subsequent coroner's inquest cited profound safety failings by the TTC.

Gunn's no-nonsense approach to the accident, coupled with his extensive experience as former manager of Amtrak, the U.S. national railway system, and having managed the New York City Transit Authority, appealed to a metro council trying to put the TTC back on the right footing.

His philosophy was to invest the TTC's resources in the upkeep and maintenance of the existing bus, streetcar, and subway network, rather than getting sidetracked with expensive new projects, such as accommodating the Luminous Veil.

Gunn's opposition to any costs he deemed unnecessary was not un-merited obstinacy. As part of its "Common Sense Revolution" platform, the Harris government downloaded most of the responsibility for public transit to municipal governments, meaning the Ontario government would no longer pay the tab for 75 percent of Toronto's transit needs.

That was a huge change in public policy, with consequences for the TTC that still persist. Money was tight at the TTC, a funding crisis only made worse with the news that the Sheppard Avenue subway line had gone over budget by $44 million, in large part because the Mike Harris government withdrew $136 million from a previous Ontario government's commitment to spend $707 million on the Sheppard subway, as reported by the *Star* on July 15, 1998.

Very Bad News

By early 1999, Birney and McCamus had become fed up with Gunn, who would retire mid-year, and several other senior TTC managers who they believed were actively interfering with the barrier project. "In our conversations or encounters with these guys, they came across as arrogant and insensitive. We blamed them for the delays," McCamus says. "But we decided against going public with our opinions in case it made matters worse."

On February 25, the *National Post* ran an article that criticized the TTC. "More than four months after city councillors unanimously approved the project, the barriers are no closer to being built and will probably not get the go-ahead in time for the coming construction season," reporter Chris Eby wrote.

"Since October, the city has been researching four reasonably priced alternatives to the Bridgemaster, including an extended crane-arm and

LASTMAN FIGHTS BACK

After becoming mayor of the newly amalgamated Toronto supercity, Lastman got into a fight with Mike Harris. "Premier, you lied," he said, over the cost of downloading services.

"Nobody likes to cut programs, and nobody likes to increase taxes. But the provincial and federal governments left us no choice," Lastman said during a state-of-the-city address in 2001. "Toronto doesn't get a damn thing and it's time that changed."

His bold approach worked: Harris eventually offered the city a $50 million grant and $200 million in interest-free loans.

In 2017, *Star* columnist Royson James, looking back at amalgamation twenty years later, wrote about that turbulent time in the city:

"By the time the amalgamated government took office on Jan. 1, 1998, the metropolis had grown weary. And Harris bludgeoned what little fight was left by turning the bazooka on the city with an unprecedented dump of service costs and cuts on the new city, rendering it almost stillborn.

"Queen's Park used to pay close to three-quarters of capital costs and half the operating costs for the TTC. Harris advised the new government it was getting out of paying the operating costs and grudgingly supplied a diminishing percentage of the cost of building the system and supplying it with vehicles."

a permanent inspection platform, but none have been approved so far. Yesterday, the commission passed a motion saying the TTC and city officials should look seriously at having a permanent inspection platform under the middle section of the Viaduct, and the outer halves could be inspected from the Don Valley Parkway and the Bayview Extension. But according to sources close to the issue, the TTC is unhappy with the design of the suicide barriers and is intent on having the current plan scrapped, which would delay matters even longer."

To Al Birney, delay was an anathema. "I wouldn't say my father was the most patient man in the world," says Mitch. "He wanted things done, and he wanted them done correctly. He didn't want any of the bureaucracy that went with it. He didn't like the committees, and he didn't like the politics of it. He just wanted to save peoples' lives."

That assessment of his father's demeanour soon became all too clear.

The Rumble in the Rotunda

When Mel Lastman was elected mayor, he entrusted Tom Jakobek with his most important election promise: no tax increases. It was a Canadian version of U.S. president George H.W. Bush's 1988 election promise: "Read my lips. No new taxes." Bush's failure to keep that pledge helped defeat him in 1992. Lastman likely knew the danger of not coming through on a memorable concept with the voters.

On choosing Jakobek to be in charge of ensuring his election promise would be kept, Lastman said, "If anyone can do it, Tom can."

"Jakobek had an intimidating presence," says McCamus. "I personally was afraid of him." Birney was aware of his reputation: "He was known for being tough and a fighter, the city's chief penny-pincher."

Before the April 30, 1999, budget committee meeting started, Birney and McCamus were told by a city staffer not to bother to speak, as all the pertinent arguments had already been made at the UED. Its vote approving $800,000 for a new Bridgemaster crane and $2.5 million for the Luminous Veil was now in the hands of the formidable Jakobek.

Birney consented, to McCamus's surprise. "I was reluctant to give up our right to speak," says McCamus. "I always assumed a hostile audience. But I didn't listen to my instincts and went along with it. It was a terrible mistake and that became obvious once Jakobek started dissecting the project with razor-sharp questions."

When the issue rose to the top of the agenda, Jakobek announced that the committee would invite speakers on the Bloor Viaduct barrier. For reasons McCamus could not decipher, Birney declined to present, waving Jakobek off.

As the debate started, Jakobek seemed agitated and the more he talked about the barrier project, and its increased cost, the more upset he seemed to become. "He tore a strip off the staff," McCamus says.

After Works staff had nervously answered his queries, Jakobek laid out his position.

"It's absolutely tragic that this project has been delayed," he said. "We know people are dying. And if it were not for that issue, I would have no hesitation saying, Go back! Send it back and start all over again because I don't know how you go from a one-and-a-half-million-dollar budget to a two-and-a-half-million-dollar budget, after a year. And there's *only one* acceptable design? And there's only one company that can build it? So, you know what? I *am* going to say that. Send it back!"

McCamus watched as his partner was becoming agitated at the prospect of one and half years of hard work being flushed down the drain.

"Al turned to me and pleaded, 'Michael, we have to say something!' I explained that we'd already forfeited our chance to speak. He sat in his seat, his face getting redder and redder," McCamus says. He was becoming concerned because Birney had a history of high blood pressure and had suffered a heart attack in the 1980s while renovating his basement.

Finally, Birney stood up, walked toward the committee tables, and interrupted the councillors. "I'd like to say something, Mr. Chairman," Birney said to Jakobek.

Jakobek was annoyed. "You know, I asked you people if you wanted to talk and you declined. And the way this place works is we listen to what you have to say and then we take it into a debate."

Birney feigned ignorance. "Well, I actually didn't understand that."

Although he wasn't obligated to bend the rules, Jakobek said, "Well, why don't you sit down and make your comment?" He had no idea what was about to come.

Birney positioned himself in front of the microphone and proceeded to give the councillors a tongue-lashing.

A *Toronto Star* article from the next day reported what he said verbatim (edited here for length):

"Mr. Chairman," said Birney. "This project has gone from one committee to another to another to another, and you're passing the buck. Just a few weeks ago, a lady jumped [at the viaduct]. Now somebody has to be responsible. There's nothing politically right that's morally wrong, and it's morally wrong to put this off and put it off and blame the architect. He had nothing to do with it.

"Obviously, you don't have mental illness in your own homes. Otherwise, you'd understand. The Bloor Street Viaduct is a magnet. You know it, and I know it. But all of a sudden, we don't know anything?

"We've sent so many faxes to each and every councillor. But we come in here, and we get the impression that no one has ever heard of this. We had suicide prevention experts, we had psychiatrists, we've had engineers, we've had the historical society. What more? Nineteen [suicides] last year. All because of bloody well bungling. And it's not right! It's not morally right to be

THE POWER OF ORATION

As Al Birney left the budget committee room, John Spears of the *Toronto Star* came up to him. He wanted to thank Birney because it was "Bring your child to work day."

"My son's been sitting here all day through one committee meeting after another," Spears said. "He must have thought his father has the most boring job in the world. Then you got up to speak, and my son sat up. He looked at you and listened to every word!"

acting this way. Make a decision. If you send this back to tender, you'll get the same thing all over again.

"Stop the suicides!" thundered Birney in a crescendo of moral indignation. "This is what's decent!"

"It was a tour de force," says McCamus. "He bowled them over with an outburst of sincerity and passion, honesty, and morality. My heart was beating like a jackrabbit's. Everybody in the room was staring at Al."

They found out later that Birney's speech had been televised live into every councillor's office.

"I loved what Al said," says McCamus. "This was exactly what needed to be said in exactly the right tenor at exactly the right time. It was a perfect expression of our feelings. He spoke for me and thousands of families of the mentally ill who had been silent for too long."

But Jakobek was not ready to concede anything to the flustered former salesman.

"Sir, I can sit in your chair and feel the way you are feeling. But can you sit in my chair and feel the way I'm feeling?" he asked.

After repeating his concerns about the new price tag and the sole-sourcing design issue, he said, "Suppose you were a city councillor, and you said, you know what? This is an important issue [but] a year and a

HARD WORK ACKNOWLEDGED

On October 5, 1999, Ontario lieutenant governor Hilary Weston invited Al Birney, Michael McCamus, and about thirty other volunteers with the Schizophrenia Society of Ontario to a private reception in the Ontario Legislative Building. The purpose was to present the SSO with a Community Volunteer Award, which she had created to honour unsung heroes in the community.

"Al and I really appreciated what she did," says McCamus, "especially because she had promoted awareness of schizophrenia and mental illness. She was the honorary patron of SSO, which was noted on its letterhead."

half later, it comes back and it's a mess. I ask you, what would your answer be?"

Birney was unchastened. "Well, Mr. Chairman, my answer would be I would have read the reports that were written about this. I wouldn't have left it until the last day and the last hour to be asking questions. The way I look at it is either these reports have been read or they've been put into file 13.

"I mean you're asking all these questions of us. These questions could have been answered six months ago."

McCamus then asked to make a deputation. Jakobek again agreed. Among the points McCamus addressed was why there was only one approved design. "The reason," he said, "is because the other barriers in the contest were scalable, climbable."

After a few councillors shared their opinions, the most amazing thing happened: Jakobek changed his mind. He said his committee would accept the UED committee's recommendations, which it did, unanimously.

"You know I've been doing this for 16 years, and sometimes you wonder if a deputation makes any difference," Jakobek said. "Well, today it did. Today it ran home." Not only did he thank Birney and McCamus, he moved that they be present at city council when it debated the issue the following month.

"I really believe that on that day," McCamus says, "Al Birney did what he was born to do. He made himself indispensable to the existence of the Bloor Viaduct suicide prevention barrier. Without Al Birney, there simply would be no Luminous Veil. It would be in the trash bin of history."

The next day, Birney got a call from a teary Mary Doucette. "You were the right man in the right place saying the right things," she told him.

On May 11, council supported the budget committee's recommendations by a vote of forty-six to two.

The battle appeared to be over. "Al had challenged city hall and won," McCamus says. "The barrier would proceed. At least, that's what we felt certain of at the time."

SANTA AL

In the late 1990s, two mental health organizations, the Canadian Mental Health Association and the Family Association for Mental Health Everywhere, partnered in Scarborough to put on a social recreational night once a month in the basement of St. Margaret in the Pines Anglican Church. It was designed as an evening for former psychiatric patients to relax and have fun with families who had shared their experience.

Al and Kathleen Birney volunteered with both organizations. Al, in particular, liked to play Santa Claus at Christmastime.

Because one of his jobs had involved selling freight to shipping companies in Scarborough, Al had a long list of contacts. As the holidays approached, he went around to all the factories and shippers he knew asking for in-kind donations, such as coloured pencils and pens, stationary, notebooks, socks, hair combs, toothpaste and toothbrushes, plastic wallets, baseball caps, T-shirts, sunglasses, plastic cups, and little toys.

"He'd spend forever down in the basement, wrapping all the presents," says Mitch. "And he'd get the ladies from the Greek Orthodox church, and they would make all the soup. They were awesome. They could really cook. I would show up, and I'd have my guitar, and I'd play Christmas songs."

Kathleen and some other volunteers cooked the forty or fifty attendees a Christmas dinner that included the soup, turkey, potatoes and gravy, salad, apple pie, and ice cream. Every Christmas, this group, some of whom were lonely and isolated, knew they would have a memorable evening after which they would walk home well fed, with an armful of gifts, delivered by Al dressed up as Santa Claus.

"Nothing gave Al and Kathleen greater joy," says Michael McCamus. "As Christians, they believed it was their duty to help people less fortunate than themselves, and by making other people happy, they also enjoyed great satisfaction."

13

The Project Steering Committee in Wonderland

M ichael McCamus spent the spring and summer of 1999 working for a lawn maintenance company. In his spare time, he researched crisis phones that had been installed at various suicide magnets, a project the Works committee had asked the Bloor Viaduct Project Steering Committee (PSC) to take on.

He conducted research on phones installed at the Golden Gate Bridge; the stunning 530-foot Beachy Head cliffs, in Sussex, UK; the Bridal Veil Falls (the smallest of the three falls that comprise Niagara Falls) and adjacent Horseshoe Falls in New York; the Mid-Hudson toll suspension bridge, in Poughkeepsie, New York; and the 3.4-kilometre Coronado Bridge, in San Diego.

One weekend, he travelled to Niagara Falls, New York, to take photos of the emergency phones there. "It was great to see them," he says, "but depressing to know there still weren't any at the viaduct." He also reached out to suicide prevention organizations in several other U.S. locations, as well as two in England, by email, phone, and fax. They obliged and sent him details about the logistics of their phone systems.

At summer's end McCamus presented his findings at a meeting of the PSC, hosted by Karen Letofsky and also attended by Dr. Isaac Sakinofsky and Ellis Galea Kirkland. To his shock and dismay, "the meeting went really badly," McCamus says. Sakinofsky derisively called him "an instant expert," while Letofsky said phones on the viaduct were no longer needed because the barrier would soon be completed.

"But council has approved six phones for the viaduct," McCamus countered.

Sakinofsky and Kirkland wanted to recommend council put phones and signs on the Leaside Bridge, which spanned the Don River about three and a half kilometres north of the viaduct, a proposal McCamus rejected.

"To be honest, I thought Sakinofsky, Letofsky, and Kirkland hadn't learned enough about how city hall worked," he says. "To me, it was obvious phones on the Leaside Bridge would take another six months or a year to achieve. They were throwing away the ace cards we had already been dealt: City Council had already approved phones/signs for the viaduct. All we needed to do was come up with some details, which was not difficult to do, so the Works staff could proceed to implement the phones and signs at the viaduct.

"I thought a bird in the hand [six phones for the viaduct] was better than two in the bush [asking for phones at Leaside, which had never been discussed before nor ever approved]."

He told the committee he intended to present his research to the Works committee, no matter their stance. "I've spent my whole summer researching this," he complained.

Letofsky and Kirkland bridled at his threat. He then phoned Revington and Birney, who both told him not to worry about the phones, and to "keep your eyes on the prize — the barrier."

With the matter at a stalemate, the PSC voted to shelve the phone proposal for the time being. The committee would soon have an unforeseen, and alarming, reason to put it back on the table.

Down the Civic Rabbit Hole

In late October 1999, the Works department staff presented a bombshell report on the results of a tender call for constructing the Luminous Veil.

Only three companies had bid on the contract, with the lowest, Bridgecon Construction, coming in at $5.5 million and the highest at $8.3 million. The price of the barrier was now more than $3 million over the approved budget. "But no funds are allocated for the additional expenditure," the report said.

The PSC volunteers were shocked. Dereck Revington believed the bids had escalated because the contractors were concerned that the project was a risky build and needed to cover the possibility of unforeseen costs.

DESIGN EXCELLENCE

Over the years, many prominent architects praised the Veil. Bill Chomik, of Toronto's Kasian Architecture, Interior Design and Planning, wrote: "I'm sure if Glenn Gould were alive to experience this bridge — this 'urban harp' — walking it, or even driving it, it would surely have been one of his favourite diversions."

Barry Sampson, assistant dean of the University of Toronto's Faculty of Architecture, Landscape and Design, wrote: "The design accomplishes one of the most difficult tasks, adding to an historical monument and satisfying needs never imagined within the notions of civility that inspired the original bridge designers."

Unsurprisingly, the Veil won numerous awards: a Canadian Architect Award of Excellence (1999); Canadian Mental Health Association Achievement Award for the project's contribution to public discourse concerning mental health and the design of cities (2003); and a Canadian Institute Construction Steel Design Award for Innovative Engineering (2003). After the LED displays were added, the Luminous Veil won a DARC Award (Decorative Lighting in Architecture) for Best Light Art Scheme (2017); and a City of Toronto Urban Design Award of Excellence (2019), presented to Dereck Revington Studio, artist and prime consultant; Mulvey & Banani, lighting and electrical engineers; and Blackwell Structural Engineers.

As a result of the report, the city's commissioner of Works and Emergency Services recommended cancelling the tender call for the installation of the "safety fence." The commissioner wanted the authority to issue a new "request for proposals" with a maximum budget of $2.5 million. "That would sound the death knell for the Dereck Revington Studios/Yolles Partnership model that council approved following a design competition more than a year ago," a *National Post* story noted.

"These people can spend a year just sitting around looking at pictures and commenting on them," an infuriated Al Birney said to the *National Post*. "Too much time has already been burned up. We have to get something up right away. Why not bite the bullet and carry on?

"If it was any other group of people, they'd have something up by now. But the mentally ill, well, you can stall it and stall it. What about the 19 lives last year? What about the 22 the year before? We don't even know what the final toll will be this year."

Joe Pantalone, now retired from politics, says, "The problem was that the original budget estimate was way too low. A budget is just a budget, not the actual cost. You don't find that out until you tender. The gentleman [who came up with the original low estimate] ought to have been embarrassed, because he was a senior guy and should have known better."

Pantalone then adds what the majority of people who have dealt with projects involving the city learn all too soon: "It's always [going to cost] more than you think it's gonna be."

The following month, on November 3, the Works committee discussed the project for the first time. Its members had more than likely read a *Toronto Star* editorial published on November 1.

"The city's well-intentioned plan to build a barrier on the Bloor Viaduct … is turning into a fiasco," the editorial began. "It would be nice to have a barrier that wins design awards, but not at a price that is unaffordable. If the city can't build the barrier at a lower cost, it should scrap this design and go for something cheaper."

The editorial by the liberal newspaper deflated the members of the PSC. A letter to the committee supporting the budget for the Veil, written by Councillor Pam McConnell, helped bolster their spirits.

"I recognize that there is great concern about the significant increase in costs for this project. Starting over or moving to a temporary barrier is not the answer," she began.

"The attached estimate [from Vermeulens cost consultants] shows that almost $2 million of the cost overrun is from non-structural costs. These

PROMINENT PEOPLE DISCLOSE PRIVATE TRAGEDY

Although the spirits of the barrier campaign volunteers were seriously dampened in October 1999, a private event, which was attended by a few invited reporters, helped to boost them.

In the middle of the month, Dr. Paul Links and Doris Sommer-Rotenberg of the University of Toronto's Arthur Sommer Rotenberg Chair in Suicide Studies invited several prominent Canadians to share their experiences with suicide.

Former Canadian heavyweight boxer George Chuvalo told the audience of how he lost his wife, Lynne, and his son, Jesse, to suicide. Two other sons, George Jr. and Steven, both died of drug overdoses.

Ryerson University vice-president Gordon Cressy (a former city councillor) talked about his younger brother, Bill, who killed himself by jumping from the third-floor window of Sunnybrook Hospital after being admitted for psychiatric treatment, and of his brother Jim, "who has lived courageously with schizophrenia since age 22," Gordon said. In 2023, Jim turned seventy-two years old.

Writer David Gilmour revealed that his mother had, for twenty years, hidden the fact that his father, John, had killed himself. Rather, she had said he had died of a heart attack.

Former finance minister Michael Wilson spoke about losing his son, Cameron, to suicide.

Doris Sommer-Rotenberg, whose son, Arthur, had taken his own life, said suicide victims are often "faceless and nameless" and are not spoken of by their loved ones out of shame. "We need to change that attitude and demask the tragedy," she said, in explaining why she and Dr. Links had organized the event.

costs would apply to any proposal, and therefore make the $2.5 million estimate originally proposed impossible to meet under any circumstances.

"I suggest that the Committee continue to pursue the existing design and defer the matter until the Commissioner [of Works] can report on what can be done to reduce the overall cost of the existing proposal (including changes to the contract tendering process) and what can be done to raise money to offset the increased costs."

She then added a personal anecdote: "My children are enrolled in the high school at the west end of the viaduct. They have seen a lot of deaths. My daughter Maddy saw two deaths in the last three months. She has seen the mutilated bodies, one of which was found in the playing field just before gym class. Those memories will stay with her for a long time."

Nonetheless, at a January 12, 2000, meeting, the committee decided, by a vote of four to three, to cancel the Luminous Veil and hold a new design competition. In a confusing addendum, it also approved private fundraising (with no details provided) and the possibility of funding a $1.3 million plexiglass bus shelter barrier.

"Two years of our blood, sweat, and tears have just been thrown into the trash bin," an angry Al Birney said. "I've become hardened by the process." Revington said, "It can be a very soul-destroying process." He noted, however, that there was confusion within the Works committee and hoped the project could still be saved by city council.

The Mayor Steps Up

Rather than giving up, which Birney and McCamus would have been excused for doing, they represented the PSC at a news conference on January 25, 2000, at which McCamus pleaded for an emergency meeting of the PSC with Mayor Lastman. "Mayor Lastman, if you're watching, this city is teetering on the edge of an historic mistake, a mistake that could cost lives and a mistake that could deface this historic monument," he said.

The decision to press forward paid off.

Lastman agreed to the meeting, which was also attended by Mary Doucette and *Canadian Architect*'s Marco Polo. Lastman's first question to the group was "Where is it?" Ellis Kirkland explained where the Bloor Street Viaduct was located.

After much toing and froing, Lastman agreed to support the Luminous Veil design at a full city council meeting on February 2. He also liked the idea of a private fundraising initiative.

True to his word, at the February 2 meeting Lastman told councillors they should not support an inferior design just to save money. "I don't think we should settle for a chain-link fence, or a solid fence," he said. "It's a historic bridge, and I think it should look great."

Joe Pantalone also chipped in, saying those opposed to the design were looking for "a silly, chintzy thing that you would not put in your backyard."

There was considerable opposition on council. "I want something that stops people from jumping. I don't want something that looks good," Councillor Brian Ashton said. He had support from councillors Ila Bossons, Joan King, Mario Giansante, and Doug Holyday in particular, some of whom didn't want any kind of barrier whatsoever.

Bossons was a peculiar opponent, McCamus thought. She had been one of the four who voted to cancel the Veil at the Works committee. "If she had supported it, the vote would have been four to three in our favour," he says. "During this long process, she really got up my nose."

The *Star* called her an "independent progressive" on her death in 2020, at age eighty-three. "Bossons was an early champion of recycling and efforts to get commuters out of their cars and onto transit or, like her, onto a bike. On Toronto council she worked with the conservation authority to protect ravines and pushed the Ontario government to let the city use red-light cameras."

Why would a progressive side with the anti-barrier members of council on this matter, he wondered?

McCamus was especially annoyed at something she said publicly on more than one occasion, including in *Never Coming Back*, the May 2001 TVO documentary about suicide on the Bloor Viaduct.

"She talked about a friend who committed suicide because she suffered from terrible migraines all her life," McCamus said. "Then she added, 'I wouldn't have stopped her. The pain ultimately depressed her.' I found that so shocking since migraines are treatable and survivable."

Despite the bellyaching of opponents like Bossons, Lastman managed to get council to approve a compromise, the seeming lifeblood of politics. ("Compromise is the best and cheapest lawyer," writer Robert Louis Stevenson once said.) The $2.5 million budget for the Veil would still be allocated, but with one astonishing proviso: The PSC would have to fundraise the additional $3 million required to build it.

After council voted in favour of Lastman's motion for a fundraising campaign, the mayor drew their attention to Birney and McCamus seated in the public gallery of Council Chamber. Most of the councillors broke into a loud round of applause. Then reporters created a scrum around the two volunteers and started peppering them with questions: "How are you going to raise the money? What are your plans? How long will it take?"

Joe Pantalone's motion to request that Bell Canada pay for the installation of emergency phones on the viaduct, a prospect now endorsed by the PSC, also passed. Bell Canada later declined. (Four pay phones were installed between February and June 2000; a person could connect with the Distress Centres toll free. They have since been removed.)

As McCamus and Birney drove home from the meeting, they anxiously mulled over what had just happened. "I said to Al, 'We're the face of the PSC. If we can't raise the money, they're gonna say, Birney and McCamus failed to get the funding. It died because of them.' Al was really shook up because at the Schizophrenia Society fundraising was garage sales. On a good year we were raising maybe a few hundred thousand dollars for the whole provincial organization."

Not long after, Birney stepped down from the PSC. "The only person who can do [the fundraising] is Ellis [Kirkland]," he said. "She's the only one who's raised money of this magnitude, who has the right connections. She has to be the face of the fundraising committee."

Fortunately, Kirkland agreed. Soon after, she was elected chair of the PSC, with McCamus by her side as vice-chair.

A High-Profile Suicide

As Ellis Kirkland was engaged in her fundraising efforts, a high-profile suicide kept the topic on the city's front pages and newscasts.

At about 5:00 a.m. on June 1, 2000, a motorist on the Bloor Viaduct saw a man climb over a railing at the western end of the bridge and disappear. The driver immediately called 911. By the time police arrived, all they could do was identify and remove the broken body that lay fifty-five metres (180 feet) below, disrupting traffic on the Bayview Extension.

The mangled corpse was that of prominent writer and broadcaster, H.S. Bhabra, who decided to end his life a week before his forty-fifth birthday. "There were two pages of notes tucked into his pockets," *Saturday Night* magazine reported six months later. "One note stipulated that he not be resuscitated should the leap leave him clinging to life. Another stated that he was in Canada illegally."

Although many who knew the often-belligerent artist understood that Bhabra had "a complex and troubled personality," as friend and novelist Susan Swan would write in an essay for the *Globe* later in the month, they were likely unaware of the extent of his demons.

He would cut off contact with close friends for extended periods of time, she wrote, as one example.

Born in Bombay (now Mumbai), India, in June 1955, his family moved to England when he was two years old. An exceptional grammar school student, he won a scholarship to Trinity College Oxford, graduating with a degree in English Literature.

He worked in financial advertising in the City of London for more than five years, before resigning in 1984 to finish a novel, *Gestures*, which he'd been struggling to complete for many years.

The novel is a fictional autobiography of eighty-three-year-old Jeremy Burnham, an English career diplomat. It begins in Venice in the 1920s, as Mussolini and his National Fascist Party come to power. The young foreign service officer meets an attractive older woman and several of her friends. One of them is brutally murdered. It ends in post-war Amsterdam, which is reeling from the ravages of the war. The book's jacket describes it as "a richly wrought narrative of a world caught in the flux of the twentieth century."

In 1987, *Gestures* won a Betty Trask Award, awarded to a writer under the age of thirty-five for their first novel. It was a dazzling debut; it also turned out to be the only book written under his name. In the next few years, he published three thrillers: *The Adversary* and *Bad Money* under the pseudonym A.M. Kabal, and *Zero Yield* under the name John Ford.

Following a stint in Los Angeles, where he was unable to forge a career as a screenwriter (he did win twenty-two thousand dollars on *Jeopardy!*), Bhabra moved to Toronto in 1994, where his parents lived at the time.

Before long, the erudite, humorous, and opinionated writer became a well-known fixture in the city's literary community. He taught at the Humber School for Writers, then soon after, in 1995, became a co-host of TVO's program about books, *Imprint*.

By all accounts, Bhabra was difficult to deal with, if not downright nasty, especially toward his first co-host, writer Marni Jackson. He made it clear he considered himself the only person suited for the hosting chair; self-aggrandizement was one of his common traits. In 1997, his contract was not renewed. (In 2014, Jackson would accuse him of having sexually harassed her during her time on the show.)

The next few years proved to be a struggle for Bhabra to earn money. He did some freelance writing, rarely a lucrative endeavour, then landed a position on an arts show, *Ôzone*, on TFO, the French-language equivalent of TVO (he was fluent in French). But artistic differences, a recurring theme, led to him leaving the network in 1999.

His friends saw one glimmer of hope, however, and it had the potential to be a big one: He said he was working on a one-million-word quartet of novels (*South*, *West*, *North*, and *East*) featuring Jeremy Burnham as the central character. "In typically grand manner, Bhabra informed friends that he had the Nobel Prize for Literature in his sights," *Saturday Night* reported.

It was not to be. "Bhabra had taken a 5,000-word outline for *South*, as well as a draft of the first fifty or so pages, to [editor] John Pearce at Doubleday," the magazine said. "'It was in the spring of 1999,' remembers Pearce. 'He said he needed the contract within the next ten days, and that he was desperate and in a financial crisis.' Dates are uncertain but it appears that this was around the time that Bhabra had moved in with [Vee] Ledson, who agreed to support him for an unspecified period as he worked to complete his novel." When he died, it was reported Bhabra owed her thirty-three thousand dollars.

"The outline for the first novel of the quartet, *South*, was confusing and lacking in conviction," *Saturday Night* said. "The sample chapters were rough, and though Pearce thought they showed promise and encouraged him to keep working on the novel, he was unable to offer Bhabra a guaranteed contract. As far as we know, Bhabra never wrote another word of fiction after this; there was no evidence on his computer files to indicate that he edited or added anything to the fifty-page excerpt after early 1999."

In deep debt, overcome with writer's block, and grappling with a sense of artistic failure, by May 2000, Bhabra had made plans to end his life. He spent the day before his death writing suicide notes to friends, which he mailed. They would arrive after his death, which some considered a cruel thing to do.

He left a plastic bag on Ledson's front porch. In it was a confessional letter, admitting everything about him was a lie, the *Globe* reported. "He tells her he was not a legal immigrant. That there is no book, no publisher, no money [he had told her a lot of money was forthcoming]. That he failed at everything and everybody. And that he's sorry, but he has to go."

His friend, TVO's Wodek Szemberg, remembers telling *Saturday Night* about a TVO segment taped two days after Bhabra signed on to *Imprint*. Bhabra called a psychic and fibbed slightly, saying he'd just been offered an amazing, prestigious job and wondered if he should accept it. Sounding worried, the psychic said, "I'm just getting very bad feelings around it, a sense of defeat," a response that stunned Bhabra, considering how euphoric he was feeling about the big opportunity he had already accepted.

"He laughed it off," Szemberg says, "and we went on, you know, with our lives. But what's interesting is that the fortune teller was right to warn him about the unfortunate consequences [that later emerged]."

A few weeks after his death, Susan Swan wondered, in her opinion piece for the *Globe*, if writers might be particularly susceptible to the kind of despair that can lead to suicide. In response to friends who had said he was "no different from a day trader or greengrocer who despairs after a downturn in business … I felt [they] were denying the dark side of the writer's life — the entrails of narcissism, fear and paranoia.

"Whatever Bhabra's personal problems, he was living inside the vanity field that accompanies the literary life, that fog of foundering dreams and shifting perceptions where the writer's reputation rises and falls like a commodity stock. I know of no writer, myself included, who is not affected by this phantasmagoria of hopes and fears."

If her notions are accurate, those who live with writers should keep a close eye on their loved one's mental state, to see if they need support. They should also keep in mind what the American wit, Dorothy Parker, once said: "If you have any young friends who aspire to become writers, the second greatest favor you can do for them is to present them with copies of *The Elements of Style*. The first greatest, of course, is to shoot them now, while they're happy."

Michael McCamus wonders if Bhabra would have killed himself if the suicide barrier had been in place. "He liked the grand gesture, and the viaduct, especially with its association with another writer, Michael Ondaatje, offered him an exit performance, so to speak, that he might not have taken if it was no longer possible to jump from there."

Not long after Bhabra's death, the Killinger-Johnson murder-suicide also grabbed the headlines.

As the city tried to reconcile these tragic events, Ellis Kirkland had been working hard to find $3.5 million to save the Luminous Veil design. By January of 2001, she appeared to have succeeded. If only anything associated with this Byzantine story were that easy.

A FIREFIGHTER JOINS THE CAUSE

In September 2000, Michael McCamus noticed a letter to the editor of the *Star* from Ken Magill, a retired Scarborough firefighter.

Magill wrote that of the many suicides he had attended, the ones that had the most profound effect on him and his colleagues were ones when the person survived. "Sometimes it was necessary to involve the critical-incident counselling team," to assist the first responders.

Writing in support of the barrier, he said that "those who are resistant to the idea should attend one of these tragic incidents to learn how important this project is to Toronto."

McCamus recruited him, and Magill became a strong voice in the final days of the barrier campaign.

Magill subsequently appeared in the TVO documentary, *Never Coming Back*. He told the story of attending the aftermath of an attempted suicide of a woman who jumped in front a Toronto subway train and survived.

"She had a host of problems. Now she had a host of problems and no legs," he said. "And you wonder why people commit suicide? Her mother came along and said 'Where's her purse? She had thirty-eight dollars in her purse.' How sad. It was easier to deal with when they were dead.

"The one question that always entered my mind was: Could we have done more? In some cases, the answer was obvious: yes, we as a society could have done more. The CN Tower has a barrier. It's a success. You don't hear about people jumping off the CN Tower."

14

The Struggle Is Finally Over

At about 10:00 p.m. on Saturday, September 2, 2000, thirty-nine-year-old Jacqueline Corrigan was riding her bicycle along the Bloor Viaduct when she noticed a young man sitting on the railing.

She stopped and calmly asked if he was okay. He said nothing, she later told the *Globe*, "only looked at her with tears streaming down his face."

As the twenty-year-old man (she would later learn his age) started to lean precariously over the bridge, Corrigan frantically tried to flag down passersby to help. No one would stop, including two men who were walking by. "That's a sad state of affairs," she later said.

Someone finally called police. When they arrived, they were able to grab the young man and take him away for observation. "She kept him preoccupied when officers arrived," said Sergeant Karl Giedroyc of 53 Division. "I think she was instrumental in saving his life."

At Corrigan's funeral in July 2022 — she died of cancer at the age of sixty-one — her sister Margaret said in a eulogy that the young man told her he'd just found out he had AIDS and was ashamed, especially because his father was a prominent doctor in Toronto.

The thwarted suicide prompted the *Star* to contact members of the Bloor Viaduct Project Steering Committee (PSC) for comment. Ellis Kirkland told reporter Graeme Smith that it was unlikely the man would try to take his life again. She cited a U.S. study "showing that almost everyone prevented from leaping off such 'suicide magnets' lives out their natural lives [*sic*]," he wrote.

Smith also raised a question about the status of the fundraising endeavour, which had been launched more than six months earlier. Al Birney, in his usual blunt manner, told Smith he was frustrated by how long the process was taking. "This money should have been raised by now," he said. His annoyance was partly fuelled by Kirkland's unwillingness to keep the PSC informed of who she was approaching for donations and sponsorship, and furthermore, who had declined or accepted.

Kirkland did not react well to the quote. She felt Birney was sniping at her, which indeed he was. Another person Smith contacted about the lack of progress was Tom Denes of the Works department and the PSC, who demanded a status report from Kirkland.

TOOKER GOMBERG

Mel Lastman easily won re-election as mayor in November 2000, garnering almost 80 percent of the vote. Howard Moscoe, Joe Pantalone, Case Ootes, and Jack Layton were all returned to office. Tom Jakobek, Ila Bossons, and Joan King, the latter two being opponents of the barrier project, chose not to run. Future mayor David Miller narrowly defeated Bill Saundercook, another Veil opponent, for a seat on council.

Four years after the election, on March 4, 2004, Lastman's main opponent in 2000, former Edmonton city councillor and environmental activist Tooker Gomberg, jumped off the Angus L. Macdonald Bridge, a suicide magnet in its own right, in Halifax.

The forty-eight-year-old left a note to his partner, Angela Bischoff, saying he "had lost his chutzpah." His bicycle and helmet were found on the bridge. His body was never recovered. She believed an antidepressant he'd been taking, which had been linked to the risk of suicide, contributed to his death.

In 2009, Halifax council approved the installation of suicide barriers on the bridge, a process that was completed in 2010.

To her credit, on January 18, 2001, at the city's Policy and Finance Committee, Kirkland made a major announcement: She had negotiated a fifteen-year deal with Tribar Industries, a manufacturer of leading-edge LED, colour video display technology, to place two large video billboards — 8.3 metres (27 feet) wide by 14.7 metres (48 feet) high or, as the *Star* said, "about the size of two semi-trailers sitting on their ends side by side" — on the heavily travelled Don Valley Parkway (at Wynford Drive), in return for the $3.5 million needed to help pay for the Luminous Veil.

The Tribar coup was one of the last significant contributions Kirkland would make to the PSC. She would, however, make headlines in the years ahead, but not in a way anyone who knew her could have ever imagined.

Although there was considerable opposition to the Tribar deal — competitor Pattison Outdoor Advertising complained that the contract, which could earn Tribar five hundred thousand dollars a year, should have been tendered — in late February 2001, the Works committee voted unanimously to approve it. Councillor Doug Holyday was especially disappointed with the decision, which violated a no-sign promise that had been made when the parkway had been built. "I just see this as the thin edge of the wedge," he said. "And once we've let two of them in there, what's to say we won't have four or six or whatever?"

Councillor Betty Disero, who had become chair of the Works committee, reassured him the floodgates would not be opened in terms of allowing more signs on the Don Valley Parkway. The bylaw amendment required to permit the signs, she said, was "site specific."

More Distractions

When the Tribar proposal went before council on March 7, 2001, even some supporters of the barrier expressed reservations. Councillor Michael Prue, who had advocated for it since the day he first met with Birney and McCamus, worried that video billboards could cause distractions, and in turn, car accidents.

A lawyer for a ratepayer's group living near the proposed Tribar sign locations (at the Don Valley Parkway and Wynford Drive), contacted the

ROB FORD RANTS

In 2001, columnist Don Wanagas of the *National Post* wrote that there were "four dreaded words" at a council meeting: "Councillor Ford to speak."

On March 7, 2001, Rob Ford, who had first been elected in 2000, went on another customary rant.

During the debate over whether council should approve the Tribar deal, the future mayor said that putting up a fence on one bridge would lead to people asking for fences on a million other bridges.

Arguing against funding the Veil, Ford said the city should use the money to prosecute child molesters, "who are the main cause of people jumping off bridges."

city to register opposition. The councillor for that neighbourhood, Denzil Minnan-Wong, vehemently opposed having the billboards at that location, and he said so at the March 7 council meeting.

Near the end of the debate, Birney and McCamus, who had been in the public gallery, confronted Minnan-Wong as he left his council seat. They asked why he hadn't registered his opposition to all the billboards along the Gardiner Expressway if signs were so objectionable to him. "I wasn't on council then," Minnan-Wong said.

"You couldn't write a letter? You couldn't say something?" McCamus said, an angry, accusatory tone in his voice.

Minnan-Wong didn't like being challenged. The two men quickly became embroiled in a verbal sparring match. "You expect me to go to every fucking meeting?!" Minnan-Wong shouted at McCamus at one point.

"We go to every fucking meeting!" McCamus countered. "We've been to forty-eight meetings about this project." Minnan-Wong stormed out of the council chamber.

"He never thought you'd say fuck back to him," Birney said to his young partner.

THE POLICE SAY NO

In March 2001, a report by Toronto's chief of police on the traffic safety of the proposed Tribar video billboards was considered by the Toronto Police Services Board, the civilian oversight committee.

The report recommended that moving video images not be allowed on roadsides, for fear of distracting drivers. Jacqueline Corrigan, who had become actively involved with the Bloor Viaduct Project Steering Committee, and Michael McCamus, spoke to the board and asked them to delete that recommendation from the report. They refused and sent the chief's report to city council as information.

Despite other concerns about the signage concept, council voted to accept the deal, with a proviso — the city was to explore other sites for the ads. "We won!" Jack Layton yelled, as he shook Al Birney's hand.

Also present was Imants Kruze, Martin's father. "It's not only for our family but for any child — the one child you can save, and that's all we want," he said. The partner of H.S. Bhabra, Vee Ledson, who had joined the barrier campaign, was also in attendance. "I'm looking forward to it being put up to prevent further deaths," she said.

Minnan-Wong softened his stance a few weeks later when the Works department and Tribar decided Tribar could generate enough revenue if two small billboards were located on the Allen Expressway and Wilson Avenue and one giant video billboard near the SkyDome (now known as the Rogers Centre).

With the problem removed from his ward, Minnan-Wong ended his opposition to the Tribar deal. "As long as the barrier goes up. That's the most important thing," he said.

Those new sign locations had to be approved at Joe Pantalone's Planning and Transportation committee in early June 2001, and again at full council on June 28, 2001. A ratepayer's group near SkyDome contacted the city and said they didn't want the sign near their condominium, as it would ruin their view.

John Chiappetta, Tribar's president, was becoming increasingly frustrated. He proposed several other sites but continued to encounter opposition from politicians, city bureaucrats, and local activists. With the private funding no longer guaranteed, the barrier project once again seemed doomed.

A Sleight-of-Hand Victory

Councillor Joe Pantalone really liked Al Birney. "I can still see him, you know. It almost brings tears to my eyes, to tell you the truth," he says. "The way he was such a human guy, just like your favourite grandfather."

Pantalone also believed Birney's obsession with getting a barrier installed on the viaduct was a righteous undertaking. "I understood his frustration at how long this important decision was taking," he says.

Although Birney appreciated Pantalone's support, he worried that the other councillors were getting tired of having to deal with him and McCamus. "More than once, Al said familiarity breeds contempt," McCamus says. "He said: 'We've been in these peoples' faces for years, they're not gonna like us forever, and some of them already hate us.' Al had the feeling that we couldn't just keep coming back again and again and again and again."

They both feared that prediction could come true when council met in late June to, once again, consider the Luminous Veil budget. What they didn't anticipate was the deftness that Joe Pantalone would display.

On June 28, 2001, Councillor Pantalone (who would become deputy mayor in 2003) made a motion at council to fully release the $5.5 million required to build the Veil. "My motion was a bit of sleight-of-hand," he says. "It said the community would continue to raise the other money."

A practical politician, Pantalone says he understood all along that the private fundraising initiative would never succeed. "Of course I knew it wasn't possible the community would raise all that money. Once my motion was passed, the city would have to absorb the cost."

The motion passed, thanks to "all the political capital I used," he says. "I had never seen people on the other side of issues as enemies. They were opponents. I never spit in their eye. I think that helped me get their votes." After the motion passed, councillor Joanne Flint, in reference to the five-foot-four Pantalone, said, "Today, council's shortest member stands the tallest."

It was finally over. Tribar later withdrew its offer to trade its donation in exchange for a lease on city land, meaning the entire bill for the Luminous Veil would be footed by city council.

The campaign that had begun some four years earlier seemed to have come to a satisfying end. All that remained was to get it built and illuminated. The first goal would happen in a relatively small amount of time; the other, however, would take almost fifteen years to accomplish.

Birney and McCamus were elated that the battle appeared to be over, but they knew not to uncork the champagne prematurely, considering all the setbacks they had gone through in the previous years.

They were both physically and emotionally spent.

McCamus likens what they went through to a 1978 Bruce Lee movie, *Game of Death*. "In the finale, Lee enters a house," he says. "On the first floor, he has to defeat an opponent. After he kills that opponent, he has to go up the stairs to another room where there's a second opponent. He has to fight to the death on the second floor. Then he walks up the stairs to the third floor and there's a third opponent [played by former basketball superstar Kareem Abdul-Jabbar] even worse than the first two. Although he's weakened and battered from the first two fights, Lee also fights this third opponent to the end, thus winning the game of death.

"Working on the Bloor Viaduct project was sort of like that. Al and I and the others would just get finished overcoming a seemingly insurmountable set of problems, and then another Herculean challenge would step in front of us, and we'd have to dig down deep to find the energy and ideas to overcome this opponent. We were exhausted and taxed from the previous fights, but we had to carry on. We always had to carry on. And I'm really glad we did."

MONEY WELL SPENT

Although some councillors still carped at the price tag for the Luminous Veil, a 1999 study, "The Cost of Suicide Mortality in New Brunswick," by researchers Dale Clayton and Alberto Barceló, suggested the cost of saving even one life was well worth it on economic terms, not just humanitarian ones.

"The present study estimates the economic impact of suicide deaths that occurred in New Brunswick in 1996, using the human capital approach," they wrote. "For the 94 suicide deaths reported, direct costs for health care services, autopsies, funerals and police investigations were $535,158.32.

"Indirect costs, which estimate the value of lost productivity due to premature death, had the largest economic value, of $79,353,354.56. The mean total cost estimate per suicide death in 1996 was $849,877.80.

"Although the most significant impact of a suicide death remains the loss of a human life, these results indicate that the economic cost of this public health tragedy in New Brunswick is also great. To our knowledge, this report provides the first complete cost-of-suicide analysis performed in a Canadian province."

It seemed that this data, extrapolated for Toronto, one of the most expensive cities in the world, would produce even higher dollar amounts.

15

A Vision (Partly) Realized

Toronto was about to enjoy unseasonably high temperatures — in the mid-twenties — as work on the suicide barrier finally began in mid-April 2002. "The sooner it's up, the better," Al Birney told reporters, feeling less sunny than the weather due to the many delays in getting to this point. He did like Dereck Revington's design, however: "It's elegant. A beautiful crown on that old bridge."

In a February 2003 *New York Times* article about the barrier, published as workers were assembling the Veil, Revington said, "I've been given a great opportunity to deal with life and death." He noted he had been inspired by Nicholas Temelcoff, the Ondaatje character who caught the falling nun. "A barrier needs the same kind of elegance and grace as Temelcoff."

The first task for the construction crews was to install brackets along the viaduct to support ten thousand stainless steel rods, each eight millimetres (a third of an inch) thick, which would be held in place by an angled steel frame, said Mike Laidlaw, project manager for the city engineering department. The thin rods, each five metres (16.4 feet) tall, would be spaced so closely together — 12.7 centimetres (5 inches) apart — that a person couldn't fit in between them, but they wouldn't block the view from the bridge, an important aesthetic consideration. Not adding excessive weight to the bridge was another, more practical, design and engineering requirement.

Laidlaw predicted that the work, which involved installing the rods and a framework on both sides of the half-kilometre-long viaduct, would be completed by August 2002, a highly optimistic deadline. The reality, as had been the case throughout the entire history of the project, would be considerably different.

For Dereck Revington, the first day of construction had to be bittersweet. He was obviously proud that his vision, which he'd created with the Yolles Partnership as structural engineers, was going to become a reality. But he'd also been through several years of anguish, having twice been informed that his design was being scrapped for one that almost everyone associated with the project considered inferior. "The Works department tried to have him fired two times because they'd underestimated the cost of a barrier," says Michael McCamus.

The city's cost concerns particularly irked the South African–born Revington, who also teaches architecture at the University of Waterloo. At an April 1999 Urban Environment and Development (UED) committee meeting, he had defended the increased budget estimate. "There is no fat in this project," he testified. "We wanted to have lights, and there are no lights. There is not even money for paint."

Indeed, the Luminous Veil would not be lit, as Revington had envisioned it, for more than ten years. But it would end up fulfilling most of his original concept, one that, to the articulate, soft-spoken architect, would be a significant work of art, not just a pragmatic obstacle to those driven to end their lives.

"People ask, is the Luminous Veil engineering, architecture, or art," he says at his multi-level, west-end Toronto studio, located in one of the city's first artist co-ops. "Well, it combines all of those."

Indeed, it does. Revington's challenge was onerous: meet the critical public safety requirement, championed especially by Al Birney; enhance rather than mar an iconic massive public structure; and accomplish both of those goals while creating a lasting work of art.

"The Luminous Veil brings those elements together to create a tremulous spatial fabric that extends from bank to bank on each side of the bridge," wrote Marco Polo, a professor in the Department of Architectural Science at what was then known as Ryerson University, in Toronto. His 2004 article, "The Luminous Veil: Transforming Memory and Meaning at Toronto's

'Bridge of Death'" appeared in the *Journal of the Society for the Study of Architecture in Canada*.

"A series of galvanized steel bowstring masts suspend a horizontal 'V' truss of welded rolled steel plate sixteen feet (4.87 m) above the bridge deck. That truss and the balustrade below, fitted with a wood handrail of naturally finished cultivated Brazilian Ipe [hardwood], hold in tension the Veil's oscillating double layer of stainless-steel rods and cables that create the essential barrier between the sidewalk and the valley below," he wrote.

Revington had immersed himself in music and a number of other artistic forms as he began conceiving the design. "When I'm doing a competition, I'm just drawing on everything imaginable. I'm drawing on film. I'm drawing on painting. I was reading a lot of poetry and *In the Skin of a Lion*. And this is all swirling around," he says.

"And then there's the place itself. You stand on that bridge, and you feel the presence of the bridge, with the lake on the horizon," he says. "On the one hand, you've got the rapture of being on the bridge, because

Left: A section of the Veil under construction. Right: Being installed.

A CRITIC CHANGES HIS STANCE

The *Globe and Mail* columnist John Barber was no fan of the suicide barrier in the campaign's early years. He once wrote, "Like an enterprising virus, chain-link is breaking out everywhere. It's riding on the back of a good cause."

In February 2001, as councillors debated the Tribar deal, he changed his tune in a column titled, "Bloor Bridge a Reflection of Toronto's Heroic Vision."

City council, he wrote, "is about to add a new chapter to the story of this bridge, one that fully lives up to its inspiring past. Just as the original structure anticipated a great city that was almost impossible to imagine in 1919, when there was nothing but dirt tracks and cow pasture on the other side [of the Don Valley along the Danforth, a plank road at the time], its modification will add an equally inspiring element to the future landscape of this city, one of humanity and grace.

"Many of us wondered how fences along one bridge would prevent the deaths of determined suicides with a city full of opportunities at their disposal, including several other nearby bridges. Slowly and persuasively, the advocates educated us about the nature of suicide, describing the powerful role such 'magnets' play in transforming fleeting impulses into permanent tragedies.

"We worried about an epidemic of chain-link fence on every high structure in the city — 'the last word in urban grime,' I called it at the time.

"[But] just as the Viaduct is no mere bridge, the Veil will be no grim barrier. It will be a monument that reminds us forever of our city's highest aspirations at the beginning of the new century."

An Elegant Monstrosity

In a subsequent column, "Maligned Suicide Barrier Has a Grim Grandness," published in April 2003, Barber lauded the efforts of Al Birney and other members of the Bloor Viaduct Project Steering Committee.

"The families of the mentally ill will sleep better knowing that Toronto's notorious 'suicide magnet' … has lost its deadly attraction.

"But the sales job is hardly over. Even before it can prove the value of its original function, the Luminous Veil has become a powerful hostility magnet. Almost anything bold and new rankles Toronto, but hostility to the Veil goes deeper than its lack of Edwardian filigree. Every instant expert knows that it won't work, that it's a waste of money.

"So Mr. Birney and his colleagues keep busy on the talk-show circuit, answering the same objections 'four or five thousand times' — especially the oft-expressed opinion that the Veil will succeed only in diverting would-be jumpers to other nearby bridges.

"Tirelessly they cite empirical research showing that similar barriers in other cities have cut suicides without triggering more jumps from nearby structures; they discuss the impulsivity of most suicides and tot up grim figures demonstrating the obvious lure of suicide magnets. And every time they lose the battle against the ironclad certitude of common sense.

"Its protective curtain of stainless-steel rods creates a comfortable feeling of enclosure, which stops well short of claustrophobia because the main structure is canted out and away from the edges of the bridge deck. The Non-luminous Veil is a clever, even elegant monstrosity."

In the first few months of 2003, articles lauding the Veil would also appear in Reuters and in the *New York Times*, the *San Francisco Chronicle*, the *Baltimore Sun*, the design magazine *Metropolis*, and the *Tehran Times*.

it's quite beautiful, especially in strong weather. And it's also slightly terrifying. I started thinking about water, and I started thinking about the lake, and I said to myself — just this very abstract idea — I said, I'd love to bring the skin of Lake Ontario, and stretch it across the Veil, across the valley."

The music Revington was primarily listening to during the conceptualization stage was Mozart's choral mass, *Requiem*, considered the composer's final masterpiece. "I was thinking of how that kind of rhythm can be brought into the bridge and transform it," he said in 2003. "[The Veil] was conceived not as a barrier — certainly not as a memorial — but as a musical instrument."

The musical instruments the Veil brings to mind are a violin ("I see it being strung like a Stradivarius," he once said) and an aeolian harp, which is played by the wind. "The great violinist Yehudi Menuhin once wrote, 'We vibrate like the untouched violin string lying next to its neighbour, trembling in sympathy though unstroked by the bow.' The strings of the violin until tuned are slack and unresponsive," Revington said in a lecture he presented at the University of Waterloo in 2003.

"Tuned to a fine pitch they become resonant and strong. What if we strung the bridge like a violin or, more specifically, like a harp with its double row of strings? The outer row could be regularly spaced to form the barrier. The inner row could be strung in a musical counter rhythm so that when moving either on foot or by car across the bridge the strings would play against one another and appear to shimmer like wind or light on water, bringing a kind of mobility that would always keep it alive."

These ideas influenced the final design, he says. "Our task was to develop a support system that picked up the rhythm of the existing bridge structure, echoed the open 'V' of the valley and rippled like water. If we could achieve this, we could tie the composition of the Veil to the bridge, to the valley, and to the lake."

Revington's meticulous research was such that he made a video of the water in Lake Ontario — "the moving skin of the lake," as he describes it and "draw[ing] it on the bridge" — to determine the rhythmic nature of the water's movement. "There are nine different rhythmic structures that are repeated as these rods are strung out across the bridge."

"Has an architect ever described a work of this size and scope with such erudition and eloquence?" Michael McCamus asks.

Last-Minute Jumpers

As construction of the Veil continued — it would be completed some ten months behind schedule — the bridge's dark side still drew distraught people to use it as a place to end their lives. "It's a sad reality that several people have leaped to their deaths from the bridge as crews worked to build the barrier that will prevent others from doing the same," the *Star* reported.

The exact number who chose the Bloor Viaduct while the barrier was under construction is unknown. John Barber, in the *Globe*, said "construction crews working on the barrier reported regular jumps." That was echoed by the *Star*'s Jim Coyle in a January 28, 2003, column: "More than 30 people committed suicide from the bridge while its construction was being debated. People have actually jumped from it while the Veil is being built."

In a 2010 study by Sunnybrook Research Institute's Dr. Mark Sinyor, published in the *British Medical Journal*, he found there had been nineteen deaths by jumping at the viaduct in 2002 while it was being built; he offered no numbers for 2003. Since the barrier was completed in June 2003, if the 2002 total is prorated, it would suggest another ten did the same.

In the summer of 2002, however, one death was averted when construction foreman Candid Capitao pulled a man to safety. He could "see the look of terror in the eyes of the man struggling to jump from the Bloor Viaduct," the *Star* reported. "Not terror that he'd die, but awful fear that he'd live." The near tragedy made Capitao, forty-three, "want to finish the job [of building the barrier] that much quicker."

Sadly, he wasn't able to help a man who, that same summer, had a cab drive him to the halfway point of the bridge. After paying his fare, he casually hopped over the north side. Nor could he or his crew help a woman who, two hours later, "leaped to her death from the south face," the *Star* reported.

On June 30, 2003, work on the Veil came to an end. "I think the families of the mentally ill can go home at night and rest content, knowing that their children are safe from that bridge," Al Birney said. "It was something that had to be done, and we did it."

In 2005, Joe Pantalone summed up his feelings when the Veil was finally completed. "It's not a big deal anymore," he said. "It's a nonissue. It looks good. Nobody talks about it. It's one of those things where the fear of something was much greater than the reality."

Although he was extremely pleased the Veil was now in place, it wasn't the end for Dereck Revington — his creation remained unlit. Working with lighting designers and engineers at Toronto's Mulvey & Banani International, he had produced "construction documents and lighting simulations ... but, in the end, the city [said] we don't think we can persuade anyone to come up with the money," estimated to be $2.5 million. The plans were "just sitting in someone's in tray."

Nonetheless, with the barriers erected on both sides of the once infamous "bridge of death," an eighty-five-year old span that had seen more than four hundred people jump to their deaths was finally over. But its appeal remained strong. Police reported in 2003 they were getting calls about people shimmying up the rods. "It turns out they were climbing up to get a picture of the city," Toronto Staff Sergeant Tom Lynch said.

A view from below during construction.

AWARDS

Once it was apparent the Luminous Veil would finally be built, Birney and McCamus began receiving awards for their long and tireless work as advocates for the project.

In September 2001, they were presented with the Canadian Mental Health Association's Public Service Awards by its Toronto branch. Michael Wilson was the keynote speaker at the ceremony. Walter McCamus was in attendance. "I'm so proud of you," he told his son.

In June 2002, they were among the recipients of Volunteer of the Year Awards sponsored by the City of Toronto as well as the Volunteer Centre of Toronto, a non-profit organization. Deputy Mayor Case Ootes presented the awards at city hall.

In July 2002, both Birney and McCamus were flown to Alberta for the Annual General Meeting of the Schizophrenia Society of Canada (SSC), the national organization. They were given the Bill Jefferies Family Member Award. Among his many accomplishments, the recently deceased Jefferies had founded the World Schizophrenia Fellowship in 1982, which did outreach in forty-two countries. Both recipients cherished this award, because Jefferies was a courageous role model and a hero to mental health volunteers all across Canada.

Birney and McCamus especially appreciated a letter Mayor Lastman sent to the SSC congratulating the two volunteers on their award. "In February 2000, after Council approved the 'Luminous Veil' barrier design, I was pleased to lead councillors in a standing ovation for Al and Michael's efforts."

In November 2002, the Schizophrenia Society of Ontario (SSO), the organization that had "funded" the SSO Bridge Committee for two thousand dollars during the four-year campaign, honoured several volunteers. Former city councillor Gordon Cressy helped give awards to, among others, Birney, McCamus, Kathleen Birney, Mary Doucette, Joe Pantalone, retired fire captain Ken Magill, Superintendent Aidan Maher, and Abigail Tator, a reporter for the *Scarborough Mirror*.

In that same year, Al Birney won a Senior of the Year Award from the Ontario Ministry of Citizenship. He received the honour during a private gala at the Ontario Legislature. It was presented by Minister Carl DeFaria. "He was so pleased," says McCamus.

In early 2003, the Council on Suicide Prevention gave an award to Ellis Kirkland, Birney, and McCamus.

Another story, reported by the *Globe* in 2003, however, threw cold water on any celebrations the barrier proponents might have been enjoying.

The newspaper reported that in October of the previous year, there had been a bridge suicide, but not at the Bloor Viaduct. It would rattle advocates of the barrier, who didn't foresee this outcome.

On October 8, 2002, a sixty-year-old cab driver, Don Noble, "took a subway to Castle Frank station [at the western end of the bridge] at around 4 p.m. He got off and made the short walk to the infamous Bloor Street Viaduct, often dubbed the Bridge of Death. But work crews and a partially finished suicide barrier made him change his plans. He caught a bus up to

A small section of the Luminous Veil, 2008.

the nearby Leaside Bridge. Death would be quieter there. And it was," the *Globe* reported.

About three and a half kilometres north of the viaduct, and also spanning the Don Valley, the Leaside Bridge has only a waist-high railing, no deterrent to someone intent on plunging twelve and a half storeys to the ground.

Don Noble "did exactly what vocal proponents of the barrier said wouldn't happen — he went the extra distance to kill himself when the Bloor Street Viaduct became out of bounds," the *Globe* said.

"The city overreacted in an emotional way to two situations that happened in 1997," Don's cousin, Keith Noble, said, referencing the Kruze and Au Yeung deaths. "Public money shouldn't be spent as an emotional reaction to a desperate situation." He wished that money had been channelled into programs and services that "help people before they get to the point of wanting to give up on their life — not after."

This was an old refrain that would be fuelled in the immediate years following the completion of the barrier as reports came in that, contrary to what Birney, McCamus, and other members of the Bloor Viaduct Project Steering Committee had assured, people did seem to be going elsewhere to kill themselves.

Had they been wrong all along? It was a question that, like so many aspects of this story, would not be easy to answer.

THE ODD COUPLE

Al and Michael "were a match made in heaven," says Mitch. "My father used to say that Michael gave him energy. He said he took Michael's energy, because Michael was almost always up, was always going."

When McCamus struggled, perhaps because of what he had gone through with his father's illness, Mitch says, "My dad had a way of getting him to get up, and making him do things, and pushing him. It was really an incredible combination."

16

The Ironic Demise of Ellis Galea Kirkland

lmost everyone who knew the prominent architect and Bloor Viaduct Project Steering Committee (PSC) member Ellis Kirkland, including her colleagues on the suicide-barrier project, was stunned when they learned what happened on Thursday, March 10, 2016.

Apparently without provocation, sixty-year-old Kirkland had stabbed the concierge who worked in the upscale Toronto apartment building where she lived, with a large kitchen knife.

She had phoned him to request help with moving some boxes from her unit. "She was very pleasant, actually," the man, who was in his late sixties, later told the *Star* from his bed in an ICU at Sunnybrook Hospital.

"Opening the door, Kirkland, a Harvard-educated architect, ushered him toward the empty boxes down the hall, he said," the *Star* reported. "As he bent over to pick up the stack, he was stabbed in the right hip with a kitchen knife."

Kirkland continued to slash at him, making cuts on his back and one of his fingers, as he tried to fend her off. After a few seconds, he managed to escape from the unit and retreat to the building's lobby. The superintendent found him bleeding profusely and called the police.

The victim said there was no reason for the attack. "I don't really know her. Once I opened a door for her, maybe six months ago," he said. "Very strange." Fortunately, he was not badly hurt.

Before police arrived, Kirkland had fled the scene, sparking a city-wide search.

She was eventually found a short distance away, straddling an outdoor balcony on the twenty-seventh floor of the Town Inn Suites, a hotel on the northern end of Toronto's Gay Village. After Kirkland refused to surrender, two police officers rappelled down from the roof. She is said to have screamed at the officers and tried to jump from the balcony, but they successfully apprehended her without further incident.

The prominent architect was charged with attempted murder, aggravated assault, and assault with a weapon the day following the incident. She was also ordered to appear in mental health court.

"When I saw this on the news at first, I didn't believe it," Dereck Revington said in an interview. "I thought there must be two Ellis Kirklands."

When Revington realized it was the same person who had played such an important role in making his Luminous Veil become a reality, he said, "It never would have happened without Kirkland's staunch advocacy and fundraising. She [was] a woman of extreme intelligence and passion." From his perspective, "she seemed perfectly balanced and on top of the world."

An Impressive Resumé

Born in Malta in 1955, Ellis Galea arrived in Canada with her parents when she was two years old. "She comes from old-stock Maltese families, she once told a writer of a glowing profile, with her father's family tracing their lineage back to 800 AD," the *National Post* reported following her arrest. "She was born into a family of overachievers, she told a writer in the mid 1980s, with an uncle who was vice-president of the European Economic Council and another who was a Vatican theologian. Her great-grandfather designed and built an elaborate church in Italy, and his old parchment drawing of it once adorned her St. George Street consulting office."

In 1981, when she graduated from the University of Toronto's architecture faculty, there were few women in the program. She subsequently earned a master's in architecture in urban design from Harvard University with a specialty in infrastructure, for which she would eventually become known as an international specialist.

In 1987, *Canadian Woman Studies*, a York University quarterly, published a profile of her. The article noted her "passion for work" and described her as a petite workaholic: "It becomes very evident in conversation that there is nothing average about Ellis. [She] is certainly more than holding her own in such illustrious company."

"I remember when I was young, whenever I would say 'I want this,' my father would answer, 'Well, figure out how to get it, if that's what you want.' That was it. He wasn't going to give it to me. If I wanted something, I had to find out how to get it," she told the quarterly.

Toronto interior designer Sasha Josipovicz described her to the CBC as a successful, ambitious woman and a "trailblazer [who] refused to be defined by men." Her considerable success, he said, was hard won. Kirkland reached the highest echelons of her field through "tenacity and skill."

He recalled one occasion where she was carried off a plane on a stretcher. "She hadn't eaten or slept for a week while trying to close a deal in China. She managed to close the deal."

On June 5, 1989, Ellis Galea, her long brown hair twirled into two curlicued strands as they framed her beaming face, married celebrated Toronto architect J. Michael Kirkland at the wedding pavilion at Mel Lastman Square, in North York, which Michael had designed. They were the first couple to use the pavilion to exchange vows. Ellis designed her own bridal gown, with the assistance of dressmaker Nancy Fong.

Interestingly, it was Howard Moscoe who had suggested naming the square after Lastman. Some cynics, remembering the fractious relationship between the two, suggested Moscoe made the proposal to inspire Lastman to retire.

Harvard-educated like Ellis, Michael, during his career, was the recipient of a Governor General's Award for Architecture and the prestigious Rome Prize, among other accomplishments.

Following their wedding Ellis joined his architecture and design company, the Kirkland Partnership, which Michael had founded in 1978. "I think her involvement in the partnership, which did some projects on Toronto's waterfront, was what drew the city to have her consult on the suicide barrier," says Michael McCamus. "She was seen as a major player in the design community."

Kirkland's star was rising so high that she was later included in the 2003 book *Inspiring Women: A Celebration of Herstory*, by Canadian history professor Mona Holmlund and edited by Gail Youngberg. "I didn't enter the business world with any kind of notion that I wanted to be one of the establishment boys or I wanted to beat the system," she is quoted as saying. "I just wanted to find something that satisfied my desire to accomplish things in this world. Really, that's my prime motivator. I just wanted to get things done."

Kirkland's considerable accomplishments included having been a registered lobbyist for two First Nations communities, Fort Albany and Kashechewan, as well as functioning as a director and vice-president of the NATO Association of Canada, a non-profit, non-governmental organization that "strives to promote peace, prosperity and security through awareness of NATO and international relations issues."

She also spent time as chair of the Committee of Canadian Architectural Councils and, most notably, was the first woman to serve as president of the Ontario Association of Architects.

Some Concerning Matters

In early June 2017, Kirkland, who had been out on bail since May 2016, was found not criminally responsible (NCR) for the random attack. A judge ruled she was suffering from a major mental illness at the time.

All charges against her were withdrawn; she was released on bail pending a hearing by the Ontario Review Board. The board can order anyone found NCR to be discharged back into the community, subject to appropriate conditions, or can direct the person to be detained in a hospital for continued observation and treatment.

She would determine her own fate, however. On January 1, 2018,

Ellis Galea Kirkland killed herself, the manner in which was never reported.

It seemed that the tragic story of Ellis Kirkland had ended with her death on New Year's Day, 2018, but that was not the case.

In October of that year, the *Globe* reported that "Kashechewan, a fly-in community on the western shore of James Bay that is constantly being evacuated due to flooding," was going to court to try "to recoup millions of dollars it obtained through loans secured with the help of a Toronto architect who now stands accused of diverting the money to her own companies and alleged co-conspirators."

Chief Leo Friday said in a claim filed through the Ontario Supreme Court that Kirkland, and a number of her associates, had obtained, or tried to obtain, loans exceeding $11 million. That claim said that none of the defendants — there were nine companies she controlled — provided any goods or services, or any material value, to Kashechewan. The outcome of that lawsuit is currently unknown.

Not long after that story was published, someone calling himself X. Jupiter Hart published a mostly scathing account on the internet of the twelve years he says he spent working for Kirkland.

"I remember when the arrest first happened. For the next week or so, I would find myself almost snickering as I read the opinion pieces of the punditry, the ones that pondered the question of why this woman — a successful executive and infrastructure specialist who could boast a résumé more impressive than most ... and who seemingly 'had it all' — would commit such a heinous and utterly senseless crime," he wrote.

"What the majority of the public doesn't understand is that Ellis did not just wake up one morning, go insane, and stab a dude out of the blue, after a lifetime of otherwise impeccable service to the community, the nation and the world. The stabbing incident that brought her to the attention of the press was merely the culmination of a long, slow descent into madness that took place over the span of many years. A descent that I had the misfortune of witnessing personally."

Hart detailed Kirkland's many accomplishments; he also mentioned that she was a cancer survivor. "She had been declared terminally ill a total of three times and was still around to tell the tale," he wrote. "I had never met anyone like her in my life. She was like some kind of superhuman or something, like a female James Bond."

Kirkland once told him, he wrote, that "at the time she was first diagnosed with cancer (which I believe was around 1997), she was on the verge of becoming a billionaire. The cancer was a major roadblock in that career momentum. It confined her to a hospital bed for several years, putting a dent on her career prospects and her fortune."

Hart said Kirkland "was always persnickety about minor details and was all in all a difficult woman to please, but that wasn't the worst of it. When she was having a really bad day, it was not at all unusual for her to fly into a rage and utterly berate me and my work, screaming at the top of her lungs things like: 'What kind of drugs are you on? Can't you see that looks UGLY?! Are you really that fucking stupid?!'

"Sometimes, she would punctuate her rage by throwing random shit across the room, blaming me if said shit breaks. I recall several incidents where she would literally tear documents I was working on out of my hand and callously rip them up right in front of me, because fuck you, that's why. If I so much as dared to suggest that she ought to do something about her anger problem, her response, expressed in her characteristic abrasive manner loud enough to wake all of Pompeii, would invariably be something along the lines of: 'I don't have a fucking anger problem, you FUCKING asshole! I went to Harvard and you didn't, so FUCK YOU!!!'

"That's just a small sampling of the abuse she dumped on me personally. I haven't even gotten into what she did to other people yet. In the dozen years I worked for her, I would regularly witness her read the riot act to her executive assistant du jour for the high capital crime of failure to read her mind."

Despite his considerable misgivings about her behaviour, Hart said he had no regrets having worked for Kirkland, whom he admired. He theorized that her cancer scares drove her to work harder than most people. "This was a woman who lacked any ability to take a deep breath and calm down. She slept maybe two hours a night, and that was on a good night. The rest of the time, she was always on edge. All business, all the time. There was no dividing line whatsoever between her personal life and her professional life — the two were one and the same."

It's impossible to know if Hart's account is accurate. But if it holds any truth, it suggests that Kirkland had a much darker side to her, one that most people who knew her were completely unaware of.

Michael McCamus occasionally witnessed her problems. "She was a very positive contributor to our work on the PSC," he says, "but there were some signs that she was not well. She disappeared for long periods of time. She had mood swings. She once tore a strip off a Works department engineer at a PSC meeting in front of everybody, which seemed unprompted. She was definitely intemperate, occasionally getting pissed off at Al Birney and vice versa. When I found out she'd been arrested for the stabbing, I was surprised and shocked, but it was not totally out of character for her. She had anger issues and I'd seen her lose her temper. I'm pretty sure she was an undiagnosed manic-depressive."

Former Liberal MP John Nunziata, who represented Kirkland in mental health court, summed up what so many who worked on the barrier project felt after her death: "What's so tragically ironic is that she played a major role in making sure the Bloor Viaduct [barrier] was put up to prevent people from ending their life."

17

Backlash, Vindication, and Grief

I n July 2010, advocates for the installation of the Bloor Viaduct suicide barrier suffered what seemed to be a fatal blow with the publication of a study in the prestigious *British Medical Journal*, "Effect of a Barrier at Bloor Street Viaduct on Suicide Rates in Toronto: Natural Experiment," by resident physician Mark Sinyor and psychiatrist-in-chief Anthony Levitt of Toronto's Sunnybrook Health Sciences Centre, both respected researchers in the field of suicide prevention.

The results were the exact opposite of what the barrier crusaders had predicted — "No suicides occurred at Bloor Street Viaduct in the four years after the construction of a barrier; however, suicide rates by jumping in Toronto were unchanged because of a statistically significant increase in suicides by jumping from other bridges and a non-significant increase in suicides by jumping from buildings," the authors concluded.

Particularly damning was this: "There was a statistically significant increase in suicides by jumping from bridges other than the Bloor Street Viaduct."

Barrier proponents had persuasively argued over the years that many, if not most, suicidal people who went to a magnet such as the Bloor Viaduct to end their lives would, if denied access to that location, not go somewhere else, as so many disbelievers suggested. The advocates presented studies, reports, and expert opinions to back up this critical, central claim.

It now appeared they had been wrong all along, at least in the minds of those who were not directly involved in suicide prevention. "I knew something wasn't right," says Michael McCamus. "This made no sense."

The *Globe and Mail* had a different reaction to the study: Although the number of deaths from the viaduct had indeed gone to zero, "in some ways [the barrier] has also been a failure." The newspaper quoted the cousin of Donald Noble, the man who had jumped from the Leaside Bridge during the Veil's construction: "Keith Noble Figures the Bloor Viaduct Gave His Cousin Donald an Extra 10 Minutes."

While emphasizing that barriers work at suicide magnets, the study's conclusions were starkly negative:

- It is unclear whether barriers prevent suicides or simply result in people substituting one bridge for another or attempting suicide by other means.
- Suicide rates by jumping were unchanged owing to a corresponding increase in jumps from other bridges and buildings in the area.
- Therefore, barriers may not decrease suicide rates when comparable locations are available.

Mark Sinyor did concede to the *Globe* that one "tangential but important benefit is the barrier's protection of passing motorists in the Don Valley Parkway underneath." However, as a scientist, he had to respect the data. "The total number of suicides was the same, almost to the decimal."

The Werther Effect in Toronto

For seven years, opponents of the suicide barrier had Sinyor's study to support their criticism of the time, energy, and considerable money spent on the Luminous Veil.

During those years, Sinyor struggled with the implications of his findings and experienced negative reactions from others in the suicide prevention

WAS ROSIE RIGHT ALL ALONG?

A prominent critic over the years of "wasting" money on the Luminous Veil was *Star* columnist Rosie DiManno (Sue-Ann Levy of the *Toronto Sun* was likely the runner-up).

In a May 1999 column about a friend who ended her life by a drug overdose, DiManno scoffed at the attention being focused on the Bloor Viaduct: "The Viaduct has been mythologized, in a way, as the suicidal bridge of choice in Toronto — for the jumpers. I'm not exactly sure why, since it's not a location that beckons. And, frankly, it's common. Diving off the Viaduct seems to me an unimaginative statement, one final declaration to the world of unworthiness: 'I'm a nobody.' But there are dozens of bridges in Toronto, hundreds of tall buildings, millions of knives. Dying by one's own hand offers a dizzying array of choices. I remember one man who struck himself in the head with an axe. Now that takes balls."

Needless to say, her comments outraged those in the suicide prevention community — "It's hard to know where to start," said Michael McCamus. "How could you make light of such a serious mental health concern?" — but she was hardly alone in her opposition to the Veil.

The previous October, her newspaper had asked readers a phone-in poll question: "Do you think barriers on the Bloor Viaduct will reduce the number of suicides in Toronto?"

The results were overwhelmingly negative. Of the 190 respondents, 84 percent said no. In an article accompanying the results, "Suicide Barrier Termed a Futility," the *Star* published some of the comments callers made when voting:

"No. People who want to commit suicide will do it one way or another. Are we going to put barriers on all the bridges? A bit of [an] eyesore, wouldn't it be?"

"No, I think the money is better spent at the source of the problem, in healthcare improvements."

"Everybody should have the right to suicide in a free country, doctor-assisted. No mess."

"No. These poor folks need help. They'll just go jump off some other bridge or building. They should be putting this money to helping these people."

"Yes. It will reduce a certain amount of people jumping there. But if they want to commit suicide, they will find some other way."

"Yes. Perhaps seeing it [suicide] can't be done from the Viaduct will give a suicidal person a chance to reflect and rethink as they seek another height."

"No. What we need is a better mental healthcare system."

"Some people have legitimate reasons to commit suicide to get out of this wicked world. Why do we try to stop them?"

community. "It was quite a surprising finding, that a number of people criticized me for," he says. "I remember going to conferences or having email exchanges with people in the field, who would say that something was wrong with the study. My initial reaction was that I felt badly. I wanted to show that the barrier worked, but I was beholden to the data and the data showed what it showed."

In the years following publication, Sinyor became a psychiatrist and attended conferences and learned more about suicide prevention. "As time went by, I started to agree with the people who were critical of the study — that something must have been wrong with it, because it was such an outlier, in terms of the findings."

That growing doubt led him to examine data over a broader number of years than had been available for the initial study. This time, his analysis incorporated the years 2003 to 2014. What he found solved the puzzle that had been vexing him and others.

"One [discovery was] that the first four years after the barrier was erected were indeed an outlier," he says. "[But] if you just restrict to years five through nine, the barrier did exactly what was expected: it prevented almost ten deaths per year at the Bloor Viaduct, and the number of suicides in Toronto over that period of time, across the entire city, went down by almost exactly that amount. But then the issue, of course, was — that's a very puzzling finding. Why would a barrier start to kick in five years after?"

The answer he and his colleagues arrived at brought them back to the Werther effect: "We wondered about the impact of media reporting [on suicide numbers]," he says.

"When we went back and looked at the media reporting in Toronto twenty years ago, we found some very concerning findings, which were, first of all, that there were many, many media reports, more than one per week, in our media, on suicide at the Bloor Viaduct, and that many of the reports were focused on ideas such as barriers are a waste of money. That if people are intent on taking their own lives, they will find a way to do so," he says. "And, unfortunately, there were even some articles that presented other bridges as alternatives."

When asked which bridges, he declines to name them. "I don't want to perpetuate the same kind of problem."

He says some of the media reporting about the barrier was "quite unsafe and certainly didn't adhere to modern standards of how we would talk about suicide. It's difficult to demonstrate, for sure, but you know, my best hypothesis, and the one that I think is most likely to be correct, is that what you were seeing in those first few years was the barrier working, but then a transient media effect that was actually resulting in more suicides than would normally have been observed. And when the media essentially stopped talking about the issue, and stopped publicizing the idea of the Bloor Viaduct, and bridges in Toronto as places to die by suicide, the barrier started working exactly as was expected."

In June 2017, Sinyor and seven colleagues published their new study, again in the *British Medical Journal*, entitled, "Did the Suicide Barrier Work After All? Revisiting the Bloor Viaduct Natural Experiment and Its Impact on Suicide Rates in Toronto."

Among its conclusions was a strong message about the potential for the Werther effect to influence suicide rates, as they believed it had in the early years of the Luminous Veil.

"Jurisdictions contemplating barriers should consider pairing their construction with media education about best practices in reporting and the possibility of copycat deaths," the authors wrote.

"We further speculate that short-term outcomes in Toronto might have been different had the Bloor Street Viaduct barrier been accompanied by proactive messaging that dispelled common myths about suicide, emphasized that it is preventable, noted that the barrier is a sign that society cares about people contemplating suicide, and provided information about high-quality mental health care services available nearby.

SO LOGICAL

Sinyor likes to tell the story of American hip-hop artist Logic who, in 2017, wrote a song, "1-800-273-8255" (the number for the National Suicide Prevention Lifeline in the U.S. at the time), about a young gay man who was going through an emotional crisis.

"In the song, and in the music video, he's about to end his life, and then he pauses, and he thinks about it differently, and he calls a crisis line, and the chorus of the song is, 'I want to live, I want to live,'" says Sinyor.

"We did a study showing that in the month of maximum interest in the song, when it was most played [and after] he played it again at the Grammys in 2018, there were ten thousand or more calls to the lifeline, and about two hundred and forty-five fewer suicides in the U.S."

Accounts such as this suggest that talking about suicide, rather than suppressing discussions about it, could be the best way to combat what has been called an epidemic among young teens. The key, of course, is how it's communicated.

"Fortunately, or unfortunately depending on what the message is, our messages end up being a self-fulfilling prophecy," says Sinyor. "If we tell people that there's no hope, and that people are gonna do this no matter what, unfortunately you see more people dying by suicide. But the good news is that you don't have to only learn about how you might die by suicide. You can learn how to live, and how to survive. I never thought, when I started this almost twenty years ago, that that was gonna be the lesson of the Bloor Viaduct."

"Finally, researchers of future barriers should take note that transient increases in suicide deaths at other adjacent bridges may not be sustained in the long term."

In other words, be careful not to leap to conclusions, as they had in the first report.

"The barrier did have its intended effect," Sinyor told the *National Post.* "There was a decrease in deaths by jumping from bridges in Toronto by roughly the same number as the number that had previously been dying at the Bloor Viaduct, without an increase by other methods or locations."

According to his follow-up study, the average number of suicides annually in Toronto fell from 257 in the eleven years before 2003 to 234 in the eleven years after.

Sinyor told the newspaper, "Those numbers highlight the need for a wide complement of suicide prevention measures." He noted that the Canadian Mental Health Association has called for a national suicide prevention strategy, because suicide is preventable. "When people get the help that they need, recovery is not only possible from mental health problems, it's likely," a spokesperson said.

Media Reporting

After Mark Sinyor's second study was published, he became more seriously interested in messaging about suicide and mental health, in Canada and worldwide. This remains the focus of his public health work today.

A few years ago, he was involved in publishing an update of the Canadian Psychiatric Association's (CPA) recommendations for safe messaging about suicide.

"When we were first having conversations about that with journalists, there was some push back," he says. "Understandably, the journalists were saying things like, you know, it's an imposition for us to ask them to report in different ways. There was some skepticism about the degree to which these phenomena were real. And also, they tended to think that some of the recommendations weren't user-friendly."

One in particular stood out. "One of the previous iterations said to avoid exciting reporting," he says. "And the journalists pushed back and said, 'Are we gonna do boring reporting? That's not really something that we can do, on a practical level, given our, you know, our work.' And so, a lot of the work really involved meeting with the journalists and understanding what their needs were, and also conducting more research, which we've done in the last few years, to really understand these effects in more detail."

As part of the CPA update, Sinyor and his contributors, one of whom was the *Globe*'s André Picard, recommended

- ongoing collaboration between journalists and mental health professionals, acknowledging scientific evidence and the autonomy of journalists;
- all journalism schools include teaching of how to report responsibly and respectfully on the topic of suicide, including attention to issues related to ethics and social justice;
- media training for mental health professionals who are likely to be called on to comment on suicide in the press; and
- education for policy-makers and other prominent figures who may be asked to comment publicly on the topic of suicide.

For a document produced by Sunnybrook Health Sciences Centre, entitled "A Quick Guide to Recommendations for Responsible Media Reporting on Suicide Events," the advice was more specific and, in some cases, even more problematic for journalists:

- Avoid details and images of the method or how the person died by suicide … These details … may be triggering. [For the reporting of high-profile suicides, this number one recommendation might be difficult to adhere to. As the *Globe*'s André Picard has pointed out, how could that be followed if, say, the prime minister committed suicide?]

- Don't glorify any suicide deaths.... Instead celebrate the life of ... [a] famous person, not the death by suicide. [Although the celebration advice makes sense, a journalist will likely also have to try to explain why someone who seems to have so much would take their own life.]
- Always include crisis resources.
- [Use] appropriate language. Instead of 'committed,' use 'he died by suicide,' or 'took his/her life' or 'her suicide death.'
- Provide context. Don't oversimplify factors or say a single event lead to a suicide death. Suicide isn't caused by one event such as 'bullying,' it is much more complex, including multiple stressors, and mental illness is a significant contributing factor.
- Include messages of hope.... When individuals are reminded there is hope, that they matter, and that people care, they are more likely to get help.

In the past few years, numerous journalism and mental health organizations have produced guidelines, toolkits, and other resources to help the media report on suicides in a responsible manner. It is reasonable to conclude there has never been more awareness of how to cover this challenging topic.

At the same time, these resources might not be accessed by or considered applicable to the numerous individuals and websites that have no traditional journalistic affiliation, yet still report and comment on suicides, especially of famous people, widely on the internet.

"There's much more education than ever before," says Michael McCamus, "but there's still a long way to go. We can only hope that coverage continues to improve, whether in the mainstream media or on the internet."

A PHRASE TO AVOID

In August 2014, Hollis Easter, "a consultant, teacher, musician, instructional designer, and performance improvement aficionado from Burlington, VT," published an article on his website that addressed a cliché often spoken by suicide prevention professionals:

"People love the phrase 'suicide is a permanent solution to a temporary problem.' It appeals to something deep within us: our legitimate desire to have something valuable to say about the terrible cost of suicide. It feels like a good way to express our understanding that suicide is often a choice that only seems like a good idea for a brief moment, and that if you can just get through it things will often look better in the morning. The shaping of the phrase also has an appealing prosody to it, and we like the way it weaves and contrasts the ideas of what is quick and what is lasting. Many of us feel like, if we can just 'shake people out of it,' their feelings of wanting to die will go away.

"All of those feelings and ideas are legitimate …

"But I'd like to encourage you, gently, to find another way of saying it …

"People thinking about suicide hear the 'permanent solution to a temporary problem' very differently. In my post about suicide and Robin Williams … [a commenter named] Anne wrote:

"'When my psychiatrist told me that "suicide is a permanent solution to a temporary problem" I thought, yes, that is what I want. A permanent solution. No more trying different meds, talking about what I'm sad/anxious about, appointments, groups, etc. Permanent. Yay.

"'The words really didn't help, they almost encouraged me to do it. It also felt like my feelings were being minimized.'

"Anne's post underscores why the 'permanent solution' … language is dangerous: it can backfire.

"If the purpose of saying the phrase is to comfort a person who's hurting and, ideally, help them choose to stay alive, it's counterproductive to use language that some people perceive as encouraging them to die by suicide."

What to Say Instead

"Try to avoid giving advice. Focus on listening instead. Start with the feelings the person has and go from there," Easter suggested.

"Give them space to talk about why they're feeling so down, and why death feels like their best option right now. Give them time to tell you about it. Don't try to force them to feel cheerful by focusing on all the reasons they have to stay alive.

"Most people, if you give them space, will start to convince themselves that they're less sure about suicide than they thought. They'll find ambivalence. They'll talk themselves into being open to staying alive. *That's* when you support their desire to stay alive ...

"But really, just do your best to be direct in listening about suicide. Avoid catchphrases and pat advice, and just listen.

"Make it less about what you say and more about what they say."

The Death of Al Birney

Al Birney did not have to endure the stressful downs and ups resulting from the two Sinyor studies. John Albert Birney died of a heart attack on Sunday, June 18, 2006, following what, for him, was a typical act of goodwill. After having mowed his own lawn and that of two neighbours on a hot June day, he experienced chest pains, was hospitalized at Sunnybrook Health Sciences Centre in northeast Toronto, and died the next day. He was twelve days short of his seventy-sixth birthday. "He died on Father's Day," says Mitch.

A few days after Birney's death, Toronto City Council unanimously passed a motion of condolence to his family and colleagues while recognizing his singular, invaluable contribution to the success of the Luminous Veil. The motion was arranged by Stuart Green, director of communications for Mayor David Miller. A childhood friend of Mitch Birney, Green was a former city hall reporter for the *Scarborough Mirror* (and is now the Toronto Transit Commission's main spokesperson).

Green loved talking with Birney after committee meetings. "Al always had a joke or witty remark that put a smile on Stuart's face," Michael McCamus says.

Council's resolution said Birney gave to the city "a dedicated life marked by an important sense of commitment [and] a spirit of equality and fairness."

Six days after Birney's death, the *Star*'s Jim Coyle wrote a moving tribute.

"Al Birney left no small legacy to Toronto," Coyle wrote. "Doubtless he would have said the greatest of these was his family, the two sons and daughter [John, Mitchell, and Pamela], the four grandchildren he and wife

Al Birney (1930–2006).

[of 53 years] Kathleen produced," as well as his brother, Russell, and sister, Vera, who both attended his funeral from Ireland.

Three people spoke at the funeral: Mitch Birney; Al's brother, the Reverend Dr. Russell Birney, the moderator of the Presbyterian Church in Ireland; and Michael McCamus.

"I had trouble holding it in," says Mitch.

When Russell spoke, it was apparent that the gift of the gab was a family trait. He ended his eulogy saying, "I am proud to say that John Albert Birney was my brother."

What Michael McCamus did astounded those in attendance. "He gave the whole speech [that Al made to Tom Jakobek in April 1999]," says Mitch. "He had it memorized. It was incredible. He's such a great speaker."

In his article, Coyle, of course, mentioned the construction of the Luminous Veil, which he said was Birney's second-most important contribution. He then added, "The third of Birney's legacies was less tangible, neither flesh and blood nor stainless steel, but just as real and almost as important — the proof positive that one citizen, armed with a sense of moral purpose and dogged commitment, can make a difference."

As Coyle recalled Birney's fight to convince politicians to fund the barrier he cared about so much, "[Birney] found a city that spent millions of dollars each year on fireworks parties but found the notion of spending a few million in defence of the most vulnerable citizens too costly."

He quoted something Birney said to the *San Francisco Chronicle* for a nine-part series, "Lethal Beauty," about the Golden Gate Bridge and suicide prevention, published less than a year before Birney's death: "When a space shuttle goes up in flames, a nation goes into mourning. When the mentally ill jump, it's 'let the bastards die.'"

One part of "Lethal Beauty" focused on Birney's successful campaign to get a suicide barrier on Toronto's notorious bridge, compared to San Francisco's Golden Gate, which didn't have one. "The difference in Toronto was a champion for the cause," it said. "Birney."

When Michael McCamus read Coyle's column, "I cried and cried," he says.

When Birney recruited the young journalism student in June 1997, McCamus had no idea "we would become such close friends and colleagues.

A PERMANENT TRIBUTE

In late July 2007, Mayor David Miller and Deputy Mayor Joe Pantalone dedicated a royal blue plaque to Al Birney's memory, a gesture initiated by Stuart Green. Michael McCamus, as well as other friends and family, was present.

Located on the northeast corner of the Bloor Viaduct in a parkette called Playter Gardens, it reads, In part: "The determination shown by Mr. Birney and all those who worked to have the Veil erected shall never be forgotten."

Mitch Birney made "a little speech," he says. "That was a heartbreaker one, holy moly. I couldn't have been prouder of him."

When McCamus spoke at the unveiling, he recalled his colleague's fiery oratory, but also his refusal to give up, a quality both men shared. Yes, the Veil exists, McCamus said, but don't forget the long struggle to accomplish that goal:

"It took six years and six months, personal visits to all fifty-eight Toronto councillors and the mayor, three votes at the budget committee, three votes at the urban development committee, three votes at the works committee, two votes at the TTC, one vote at Heritage Toronto, one national design competition, two news conferences, fourteen radio interviews, 220 newspaper articles, 116 letters to city hall, 118 faxes, a $3.5 million fundraising campaign, and six separate votes at Toronto city council."

It was an especially emotional day for Kathleen Birney. "Of all the people in this world, we couldn't believe it would be him who had done something big like this. He was just a salesman, although a very good one," she says.

Also in 2007, Karen Letofsky was named a member of the Order of Canada for her work on suicide prevention.

For years we were eating, drinking, sleeping, and breathing the Bloor Viaduct barrier together. We took responsibility for that as if it would rise or fall based on our actions.

"During that time, Al taught me about courage and determination. He taught me how to be a man. He taught me about keeping promises to yourself and to people depending on you.

"If there's anything I'd want people to know about him it's this: Al Birney had the exceptional capacity to change people's hearts and minds with his words, his passion, and his determination never to give up. He made a mark on the world and a mark on my heart that will never be forgotten.

"It wasn't until his funeral that I realized — it just suddenly hit me — that Al loved me, and I loved him. But we'd never spoken those words to

The sign remains (2023) despite the Luminous Veil.

each other. When we were standing in the church, I blurted out to his son, Mitchell: 'He loved me, didn't he?' Mitchell looked at me with disbelief: 'Yes, of course. Even more than that,' he said.

"I thank God I had the good fortune to meet Al Birney at that SSO meeting in June 1997. Was it luck, fate, destiny, or divine intervention? I'll likely never know, but what an adventure he took me on."

John Albert Birney was buried in the cemetery of St. Margaret's in the Pines Anglican Church, a short walk from the church basement where he used to play Santa Claus.

18

The Veil Is Finally Lit

There's an irony behind Toronto's decision to finally spend the money to light up the Luminous Veil at night, as architect Dereck Revington had originally envisioned.

In January 2000, when the Works committee balked at the $5.5 million budget to build the Veil and suggested, instead, a bus shelter–style barricade — at a much cheaper cost — Revington blasted the decision.

"If Toronto seriously considers itself an international city — we want to go after an Olympics bid — and now they contemplate putting up a bus shelter on a historic monument, then forget it," he fumed. "In European cities, this kind of initiative [the search for cheaper options] would be scorned."

At the time, Toronto had a budget of $20 million to campaign for the right to host the 2008 Summer Olympics (Beijing was awarded the Games; Toronto's costs, of course, were never recovered).

In 2013, ten years after construction of the Veil had finally been completed, Toronto City Council's Executive Committee approved the $2.8 million required to light it up at night, using LED technology, a less expensive technology than was available in 2003.

The impetus? To make the city more attractive when it hosted the 2015 Pan American Games and Parapan American Games. Specifically, the lights would play a supporting role in a pre-Games celebration, which included the arrival of the torch relay on the Viaduct a week before the Games were set to begin in mid-July.

Revington had been correct in 2000: When it came to sporting projects, money could always be found.

True to the history of the barrier, in January 2015 city staff asked the Executive Committee for an additional $1 million, bringing the total cost to $3.8 million, in order to complete the initiative on time. Despite concerns by newly elected mayor John Tory — "I am still troubled, and I'll put it no stronger than that, by instances where we spend money on these kinds of things, which are very nice to have, when we're having discussions about our inability to pay for, whether it's adequate homeless shelter, fixing potholes, all kinds of things," he told reporters — council approved the funding (it was taken from money saved on road resurfacing for the Games).

Councillor Paula Fletcher, on the other hand, was an avid supporter of lighting the Veil, saying the cost was "well worth it." She told the *Toronto Sun*: "This is a project for the whole city, indeed for the whole region. Who doesn't go on the Don Valley Parkway? The project will light up this architectural wonder, providing an iconic image for the Games that everyone can see when they drive down the Don Valley Parkway."

Councillor Pam McConnell, who had once derided how the Veil looked, now said that it would never come to life unless the lights were added. "Sometimes you have to do what is necessary to live, and at the same time you have to have the right of beauty," she said.

Jennifer Jones, a dance teacher and chair of the bridge committee of the Danforth Business Improvement Association, had been an outspoken champion of illuminating the Veil over many years. "The most delicious part about this whole project has been the reaction and the support from everywhere we go," she said. "Everyone's so excited. There's this clear sense that the city needs this."

Lighting the Veil, to columnist Rosie DiManno, however, was money not well spent. Better to have applied it to "mental health services in Toronto, crisis intervention and suicide prevention programs," she wrote in the *Star* in 2014. "But it was difficult, ultimately futile, to counter the emotionalism of the barrier proponents."

A louder vocal opponent was John Clarke, founder of the Ontario Coalition Against Poverty. On an early spring evening in March of 2015, he led about a hundred people in a protest against Toronto spending money on lighting the Veil at "a time of dwindling homeless shelters and decrepit public housing," *Spacing* magazine reported. "When they reach a pedestrian overpass two kilometres south of the Bloor Viaduct, he steps in front of the congregation to vent. 'If you want to know what the priorities are of those bastards of the neoliberal city,' he yells, no microphone needed, 'look at *that*.' The protestors follow his finger to the Luminous Veil.... [A] banner is draped over the railing, imploring the cars below to push for HOMES NOT GAMES."

To Dereck Revington, who has a strong social conscience, there wasn't an either/or issue between supporting the causes Clarke fought for and the one he cared so much about — creating a major piece of public art. "That the Veil was left unfinished [without its planned lighting] speaks to how much art is underestimated by Toronto," he said.

Despite wanting the Veil illuminated, Revington says he always felt "very strongly that [it] would be, in my mind, a great accomplishment without being illuminated. I didn't want to have the resonance of the Veil too tied to lighting. It didn't have to be lit. At sunset, it just turns golden; it catches the light beautifully." Nevertheless, when the Veil was installed, he had it wired to ensure that it could be lit in the future, if that possibility ever emerged.

When he learned that day would arrive, "I was very, very happy," he says.

Once the lighting component had been approved, Revington spent countless hours "paging through drawings and simulations that he made to show the City of Toronto what his sculpture would look like if finally lit up," *Spacing* reported in July 2015. *Canadian Architect* would add, in 2016, that "Revington and his team [spent] 18 months working on the code that underlies the [35,000] moving [LED] lights," that were designed specifically for the Veil.

That work, *Spacing* said, was done "'essentially on spec,' as one City Official put it ... something nobody would do just for the money: hours of simulations showing different ways the 'ethereal' light will move in different seasons, the changes of speed and direction when wind moves across the strands and the way it will change across the hours of the day."

Spacing described Revington as "a sculptor by inclination, known for what he lovingly calls his 'crazy art projects': unconventional municipal infrastructure, often with light components." The Luminous Veil, he told the magazine, would "bring some light into … the darkness that has fallen on the bridge."

Nothing Like It in the World

Work on the lighting component began in February 2015 under the direction of Mulvey & Banani International, an engineering consulting firm, as well as Guild Electric, an electrical contractor, both Toronto-based organizations. The deadline to accomplish the complicated undertaking was a scant four months away.

The companies took on "the long-deferred task of executing Revington's vision, a 500-metre-long, LED-based lighting system that reacts to changes in wind speed and shifts colours according to the season," *Toronto Life* reported in a July 2015 article, "How the Bloor Viaduct's Luminous Veil Finally Got Itself Illuminated."

The lighting control system would use real-time data from a weather sensor located at the top of the Veil. "The bridge will be transformed into a 500-metre canvas. It's painting in time and light. It will never look the same," Revington said in a statement. "There's nothing like it in the world."

The original plan called for the five steel archways that support the subway tracks underneath the viaduct to also be illuminated by colour. "Controlled by computer, the lights [would] offer endless possibilities for special events though, in general, they will be warmer in winter and cooler in the summer months," the *Star* reported. When the $5 million cost for this was presented, however, Revington eliminated this aspect of the lighting. The Veil would indeed be lit, but still not exactly the way it had been envisaged.

One decision that made it possible to meet the tight 2015 deadline had been made twelve years earlier, when the Veil was installed. Mindful of the fact that lights may one day be added onto the structure, the original design included a V-shaped channel on the Veil that would allow LED strips to fit inside. In 2015, they were easily installed, as they clipped into metal brackets already in place.

As Revington and his team worked under their crushing deadline, some opponents of the lighting project raised concerns that it would disrupt the environment. In response, Revington and his colleagues researched ways to minimize light pollution of the night sky. "We have shielded the lights so they only focus on the bridge and don't focus on the sky," Paul Boken, a lighting designer with Mulvey & Banani, told the *Star*.

Despite the short timeline, and the occasional blast of opposition, the work was completed on time. "It was a tremendous accomplishment," Revington says.

The Luminous Night

The temperature hovered in the low twenties on the evening of July 4, 2015, as hundreds gathered on the Bloor Viaduct, which had been closed to traffic, for the official lighting of the Luminous Veil.

Entertainment for the event, which was called the Luminous Night, was provided by, among many others, the appropriately named July Talk, a Toronto-based band that had won a Juno Award for Best Alternative Album a few months earlier in the year.

At the official opening, which was attended by Kathleen Birney and her daughter Pamela, local politicians, Games organizers, Dereck Revington, Ellis Kirkland, and some families of people who had taken their own lives at the viaduct, Mayor John Tory put aside his previous concerns about the cost of lighting the Veil and honoured the project.

"The Luminous Veil is an example of how art can transform and beautify an important artery in our city," he said. "The convergence of art and technology completes the vision for the Luminous Veil that will be a lasting legacy of the Pan Am and Parapan Am Games for Toronto."

Toronto Sun columnist Sue-Ann Levy continued to gripe about the Veil and the Games. "I hate to sound like a party pooper but Saturday evening's

It's finally "luminous."

ceremony cost taxpayers a not-too-shabby $180,000, which seemed high
for the numbers assembled — less than I see at the finish line of any half
marathon I've run as of late," she wrote. "The lighting ceremony was timed
to coincide with the arrival of the torch relay in Toronto, which arrived on
the bridge last evening to make sure we knew there was connection between
this leftist pet project and the Pan Am Games."

Most of those in attendance, though, were awed by the spectacular show
that lit up the sky, which could be seen from atop the viaduct, as well as from
the Don Valley below, once the lights were turned on.

UrbanToronto said the visual display — Dereck Revington and his associate, Jonathan Tyrrell, had programmed the lights to represent the colours
of the flags of all forty-one countries competing in the Games — "danced
across the night sky almost like some electric aurora borealis."

The following year, *LD+A*, the magazine of the Illuminating Engineering
Society of North America, said, "The bridge never looks the same," in an
article entitled "A Sonata of Light":

"The colors along the Viaduct change according to season, weather
and wind. A weather station mounted on the bridge tracks temperature,
wind speed and direction, and changes the colors and movement patterns

MICHAEL McCAMUS CHANGES HIS LIFE

When the Veil was finally lit, Michael McCamus was not present. After he and Al Birney had achieved their goal of having a barrier installed on the viaduct, he decided to pursue a different career from journalism.

He enrolled at Brock University, in St. Catharines, Ontario, with the goal of becoming an accredited teacher. He graduated with a Bachelor of Education in June 2009. After finding it difficult to find a permanent teaching position in Canada, in August 2012 he moved to Vietnam, where he teaches at an adult English language learning centre in Ho Chi Minh City.

In 2015, he married a Vietnamese woman, Pham Nhat Kim Khanh, who has a master's in linguistics and teaches at the University of Humanities and Social Sciences in Ho Chi Minh City.

"I'm so happy I took the gamble to leave Canada and move to this amazing country," says McCamus, who turned fifty-two in 2023 and feels settled in a nation almost fourteen thousand kilometres from Toronto.

"I still think a lot about Canada, of course, and especially the years Al and I spent working on the barrier campaign. That time was the highlight of my life."

according to a palette programmed for each season. The palettes are somewhat counterintuitive — in the depth of winter, the bridge is a saturated blood red, a color one often associates with heat. In contrast, the bridge is bathed in blue during summer, with currents of gold that shoot through the Veil when the wind is blowing slowly, as if the wind is literally expressing itself in color. In fall, the light emulates the gold of turning leaves, making one feel as if they are surrounded by maple trees. Throughout the year, when the wind pauses in the bridge's cardinal points — north, south, east and west — the entire structure seems to shiver with light."

Alan McIntosh, senior designer at Mulvey & Banani, told the magazine, "Theoretically, the bridge is alive. You're not seeing the same thing reproduced over and over again because the wind will be a different speed at

2:00 than it will be at 3:00. The temperature will be different outside on a Wednesday from a Thursday, or on a Wednesday morning to a Wednesday afternoon, so the colors are constantly changing, and the movement is constantly changing."

As for its creator, Dereck Revington summed up his reaction in one simple thought: "From my perspective it's absolutely exquisite."

LIGHTS OUT

On a cold January evening in 2023, anyone travelling across the Bloor Viaduct would notice something was very wrong with the Luminous Veil: Almost none of the lights were on. A thin strip of red light ran horizontally along patches of the eastern end of the barrier; on the western end there were no lights on at all.

Dereck Revington says he's been in contact with the city about problems with the lights since April 2021.

It turned out that the company with the service contract to maintain the lights (Westbury National Show Systems) had declared bankruptcy; the city was in the process of establishing a new service agreement.

In March 2023, the city's media office said one reason for the problem is Toronto's climate. "The technological elements of the artwork, the LED lighting and the programming that controls it, are constantly exposed to damage.

"Staff at the City of Toronto are working with a specialized vendor to analyze and execute repair work on [the] Luminous Veil. The city hopes to undertake the necessary repairs this spring [2023]."

19

The Barrier Saved My Life

I n the twenty years since the Luminous Veil was erected, only one person has been able to circumvent the barrier and jump off the viaduct, according to Dr. Mark Sinyor in his 2017 study, "Did the Suicide Barrier Work After All?"

His office has no details of what happened other than the year it occurred: 2007. His source was the chief coroner's office. Stephanie Rea, issues manager for the office, confirmed that "the information is authentic" but was also unable to provide any other information, as "we do not have a code specific to the Bloor Viaduct." There are no media reports about what happened.

One possible exception aside, there is no question that the barrier prevented deaths. The number is unknown, of course (although Sinyor estimated about nine people a year had jumped from there prior to the Veil being erected), but perhaps one person's account can represent those who might have taken their lives if it hadn't been in place.

Jenn's Story

In 1975, when Jenn Hicks was about two and half years old, her father killed himself with a gun given to him by his uncle, who had used it in the Second World War. He had recently moved the family from North Bay to

Windsor, where he had enrolled in the Master of Social Work program at the University of Windsor. Following his death Jenn's mother took the family to Toronto, where her parents lived.

Now fifty and still living in Toronto, Hicks has an open, youthful face framed by shoulder-length hair styled in a natural soft wave. Her family, she says, always explained what happened in blunt, unemotional terms. "For as long as I can remember, it was that your daddy died, not by suicide, [but because] he shot himself in the head with a gun. And then we move on with the rest of our day."

Hicks says there was always some degree of secrecy about what had happened. Was he depressed, she wondered? "My mom said no, he was fine. They were getting along in life and then she came home and found him in the garage, kind of thing."

A few years ago, she learned that she could order the coroner's report on his death. "Apparently, according to the coroner, there were marital issues, and he was under psychiatric care, and in group therapy, which in 1975 was a huge stigma."

Her mother always minimized what had happened, she says, which would have serious repercussions for Jenn years later when she struggled with her own serious mental health issues.

"I just remember the whole time I was going through what I went through [mentally], feeling so guilty, like it was my fault, like I could choose to get myself out of this, but for some reason, I just wasn't able to."

Her struggles began when she was in her late twenties, early thirties, she says. "It was probably the best time of my life. I'm a speech pathologist and I had a dream job at a rehab centre. I couldn't have asked for a better job, and better colleagues."

She and her soon-to-be husband, Paul Kralik (a childhood friend of Michael McCamus), bought a house together. "It was an amazing time in our life," she says.

Not long after, everything changed.

"Paul's father got sick with cancer," she says, "and I began this hypervigilance around food and nutrition. I think my subconscious was saying I can't help him, but I can make sure I'm healthy. That was a way of coping with my anxiety at the time. And then I started exercising a lot. Before I knew it, I had anorexia and an exercise addiction."

Hicks says her need to exercise was a literal addiction. "Before work for several hours, at lunch time — I'd sneak out early from this dream job to do more exercise. I'd wake up in the middle of the night to exercise. I'd be doing sit-ups in car rides. If a friend wanted to see me, it had to be exercising. If Paul wanted to spend time with me, we had to be exercising. Not at a gym. Running, cycling, weightlifting in the basement, swimming, dance classes, you name it. Anything I could get my hands on."

She doesn't like to say how much weight she lost but will disclose she was "below a hundred pounds." At five foot four, she was considerably under-weight. "I was having heart problems, blood disorder, and osteopenia [lower than normal bone mass or bone mineral density]," and other problems she has since forgotten. "I remember when my doctor diagnosed me with anor-exia, I accused her of being jealous of me."

She went to several psychiatrists "but they just really wanted to shame me for the eating disorder," she says. "I had people yell at me: Look what you're doing to yourself. Why don't you just eat?"

At some point, she says, she began to burn parts of her body. "It was horrific to everyone else, but to me it just felt like a relief, really."

Other behaviours also radically changed. "I was wearing children's cloth-ing, because that's what fit me. But also, garish, colourful things. Like, pink bows in my hair. I can remember carrying stuffed animals with me, and I'm a professional, going to work. I was (a) not nourished and (b) not sleeping. I was out of my mind. I had limitless amounts of energy, and I had that sort of grandiose 'I can do anything better than anybody' attitude. Why is everyone else so weak? Look at me, I'm, like, superhuman. I can go, go, go, go, go, and, like, literally in the middle of the night, at any hour."

Eventually diagnosed as having bipolar affective disorder and hypo-mania, she convinced Kralik in June 2005 to buy a new house they couldn't afford. It was in the east end of Toronto, not far from the Bloor Viaduct.

A Fateful Night

Even though he was completely sympathetic and supportive, Kralik was having trouble understanding his wife's unusual and uncharacteristic behaviour. "He desperately wanted to help her, but didn't know what to do," McCamus says.

"One week [perhaps in late summer 2005] was particularly difficult. Jennifer was not herself," he says. "She was acting in strange and unpredictable ways. She had verbalized that her life was out of control. She had conflicting emotions. She had feelings of rage, of hating herself. Paul was not able to sleep. He was exhausted but still hypervigilant about protecting Jennifer. He found it difficult or impossible to communicate with his wife. He asked me to come over to his home to talk.

"That evening, Jennifer left the house abruptly in anger or distress. She didn't say where she was going or why she left the house, which was uncharacteristic. She just sort of rushed out the front door."

Hicks says that she came home after attending her music lessons that night and sensed she was going to be put through an intervention [McCamus and a female friend of Hicks were there, with Kralik]. "So I took off," she says. "I was a runner, so I ran and I ran and I ran."

Her long run eventually brought her to the viaduct, which she had to cross to return home. "The fact that the barrier was there that night, and on other times I was on it, saved my life," she says. "If there hadn't been that Veil there, who knows what could have happened?"

After Hicks had bolted, Kralik enlisted some neighbours to help search for her, on bikes and by foot, for fear she might do something to harm herself. Eventually, he called the police, who were there when his wife walked in the door.

"She was quiet and calm now. She seemed like her usual self," says McCamus.

"Paul, what's going on?" he remembers her asking in a calm, collected voice.

"Jenn, I didn't know where you were, or what you were doing. I was afraid," Kralik said.

"So you called the police?" she said.

"This has been very difficult for me," Kralik said to his wife, his voice full of emotion.

"Jennifer seemed to immediately understand that her actions were having consequences for her husband," McCamus says. The police asked a few more questions before they left to ensure that Jennifer was safe.

That night was but one example of the positive role Kralik played throughout his wife's struggles. "He was extremely, extremely supportive," she says. "He sounded like a therapist, not in a condescending way, but he just had this gift of being really attentive and compassionate, and he did his best to take my point of view. But it was really difficult for him."

It was also challenging for her at work. "I was going through major lows where I would be in my office crying on the floor, calling the help line, which was not available — they'd just be, like, please hold, please hold. And there were weeks upon weeks where I couldn't get out of bed and go to work. Eventually, I was put on a medical leave because of my attendance issues." She was dismissed from her job in 2006.

Hicks eventually found a psychiatrist she felt comfortable with. The woman prescribed a medication for her bipolar disorder that she warned could give Hicks a life-threatening skin rash. "I got this rash, and I was hiding it, because this whole time I was passively suicidal," she says. "I was like, great, this rash is just gonna do it for me. But I think Paul discovered it, so I went off that medication."

Her psychiatrist eventually found two medications that were effective for Hicks — Celexa, an antidepressant, and lithium, a mood stabilizer. "Once I got on them, once they kicked in, the mostly depressive feeling was just eliminated, gone," she says. At one point, she asked her GP if she should consider coming off the medications. "You were the sickest patient I've ever had," her doctor said. "Why would you chance it?"

Hicks has been functioning well in the years since she found the right medication. "I experience low periods two or three times per year," she says, "but they are nothing like the deep darkness of my pre-medicated days."

Ever active, she holds several related jobs. "I am still a speech language pathologist, through my private practice. I primarily see people who had had strokes or have had a traumatic brain injury of some sort or another, often at work. In that role, I also do work in the court system [helping] people who have communication disorders, who are involved in the court system," she says.

She is also an accredited Nia teacher, which she describes as "a combination of dance, martial arts, and healing arts. It's like a barefoot, standing aerobic kind of practice. Non-impact." As well, she co-created the Good Conversations, which uses the arts "to positively connect with people with a wide range of strengths and challenges, both physical and neurological, including many different types of dementia," such as early-onset Alzheimer's.

Hicks now connects her mental health struggles with her father's suicide and how her mother, a devout member of the Salvation Army, was not equipped to deal with it. "Nowadays, kids would be in therapy if their dad died by suicide, right? But back then, it was just like, get on with life. And for my mom, too. She told me her own mother said to her, 'it's time to just move on.'"

Thinking back to the night when she believes the Luminous Veil kept her from making a rash decision, she says, "I am so thankful to be here and that my behaviour didn't lead to my death. I couldn't have imagined it when I was ill, but my life has continued to get brighter and more hopeful as time has gone on."

Mark's Story

Although it was on a bridge in Sydney, Nova Scotia, not on Toronto's Bloor Viaduct, Mark Henick also knows what it's like to come close to ending his life. He shares his message of hope in his 2021 book, *So-Called Normal: A Memoir of Family, Depression and Resilience.*

"This is the end. I'm sure of it. At least, I think I'm sure. I don't want to die. It's just that dying is sort of a non-negotiable part of killing yourself. I have no choice. It feels like nobody can help me, however much they tried, or tried to try. I tried too, for a while. I can't anymore. I can't live like this."

These are the first words in his book, a follow-up of sorts to his incredibly successful 2014 TEDx Talk, "Why We Need to Talk About Suicide," which, by early 2023, had just under seven million views. Comedian Rosie O'Donnell, one of the Talk's admirers, wrote a cover quote for his book: "A peek inside the mind of someone who journeyed through mental illness and found hope on the other side."

The incident Henick described at the start of his book took place around midnight on the overpass of a bridge in Sydney, in 2002, when he was fifteen years old. It was a cold winter's night, and he was determined to end the mental pain within him, which was exacerbated by an unhappy home life with his mother and stepfather, as well as the bullying he experienced at school. This would not be his first or only attempt at suicide.

He could see his grandmother's home from where he stood, "a duplex, a company house, next to the former property of the Sydney Steel Plant," once a powerful economic force in the Cape Breton region — "the lifeblood of my hometown," Henick calls it — that closed in 1988. By the time he was ready to jump off the bridge, "it was abandoned [and] was a toxic waste site ... so I [felt] like I really connected with that place."

He climbed over the bridge's railing, holding onto it from behind, and stared at the ground some fifty feet below. He saw a rusted-out chain-link fence topped by three strings of barbed wire and wondered how far out he'd have to jump to avoid landing on it.

As Henick grappled with his lingering uncertainty, someone watching from a nearby gathering of gawkers yelled, "Jump, you coward!"

"I let go [of the railing]," he wrote in the next sentence.

As he did, a man in a light brown jacket, who had been slowly inching toward him as he tried to talk Henick out of jumping, grabbed him around the chest and the back of his shirt. He saved Henick's life.

The man later told police, who were arriving as this happened, that Henick's body was "completely limp" as he dragged him backwards over the railing. The man helped Henick get to a waiting ambulance and then left, his identity unknown.

Henick, who is a mental health advocate, is doing well today. But it was not an overnight healing. "For me, it was a slow change, and I make a point of talking about this in my public speaking, because I think we have this romantic idea of what recovery is supposed to be like, and it's a simplistic idea," he says.

"I think it's partly perpetuated by this myth that mental health and physical health are exactly the same. They're not. But it's this idea that if you get your injection, i.e., treatment, that you'll get better. And that's not how it works. It's not this hallelujah redemption moment that changes everything. It takes work; recovery is work."

A central part of his recovery occurred thirteen years later, in early 2015, when he was twenty-seven. Henick realized he needed to connect with the man who had saved him. On the advice of the *Globe*'s André Picard, whom he had reached out to, he launched a social media campaign asking for help to locate the stranger.

Incredibly, at the same time as Henick began his search, the man, thirty-seven-year-old Mike Richey, had come across Henick's TEDx Talk. "Listening to Mark speak was, like, all of a sudden, I was back on that overpass with him," he said in an interview. "And it was incredibly emotional to see him and where he's come in his life and what he's done with his life and not knowing all these years."

Richey was literally in the process of writing a letter to Henick when he was told about Henick's search for him. About a week later, Henick received a message from Richey, who lives in Halifax and, interestingly, is a caseworker at a non-profit residential facility for at-risk youth.

The two exchanged emails and eventually met in Toronto, courtesy of Henick, in May of that year.

Admittedly shy, Richey says he's so happy with how Henick has turned his life around. "He's come so far, he looks great, healthy, and happy. It's the complete polar opposite of the face I saw that night on the bridge ... he's doing great things."

For Henick, meeting Richey was like "bringing something full circle." After he'd done the TEDx Talk, people had begun reaching out to him, saying that through his words, he was helping them, that he was their stranger.

However, their encouraging words had made him wonder, "Did I make this guy [who saved him] up? Was he just sort of a story mechanism, to make my own story make sense? I started to feel this imposter syndrome, like I don't even know what I'm doing, I don't deserve this role, or these people, because I'm just a person telling my own story. So, that's what motivated me to find out who he was."

When he met Richey in Toronto, in 2015, Henick told the CBC that "to be able to actually experience this kind of closure has been incredible." He also wrote in his book that after he had found Richey, "things started to slowly turn around. Filling in this hole in my narrative made me feel more coherent, less of a fraud."

As for Richey, he says he just wanted to give Henick a hug. "It felt good, because if I could have [gone] back in time and given that young boy a hug when he needed it, that would have been awesome. But I still got to do it at the end of the day."

Just before he reconnected with Richey, Henick did something else that helped in his recovery. "I actually brought [my mother] to the place on the bridge where Mike saved my life. And that was sort of the moment where, yeah, where she was able to, I think, forgive herself for her role in my struggles. That was a transformative moment [for both of us]," he says, adding that he loved his mother despite their difficulties over the years.

These days, Henick hosts the *So-Called Normal* podcast and advocates for mental health in presentations and interviews that total in the hundreds. He also served as the youngest-ever president of a provincial Canadian Mental Health Association division.

In his advocacy role, he believes that talking publicly about suicide is essential. "There's research behind some of the premises [of media guidelines on reporting suicides], behind some of the recommendations. There's less research around the recommendations themselves, and whether or not they actually work," he says. "There's a researcher, Dr. Sally Spencer-Thomas. She's a suicidologist, a psychologist, and her concern is that it actually creates something that — these are my words, not hers — something akin to libel chill, where people see all of this stuff, all of the risks around suicide contagion, and they take it too far. They almost take it too seriously."

Henick believes that "we do need to talk publicly about suicide, and I've been one of the most vocal people on that front, but we need to do it with a recovery focus, with a message of hope that resources are available. I absolutely think we should talk more about suicide, because the fact is, you're not going to give people the idea, or plant the need in their mind. But you might reveal that it's already there, and that's a good thing. We want to know if people are suicidal. Because if we know, that's the first doorway to help."

It's About Hope

Much has changed since Al Birney and Michael McCamus began their quest to convince the City of Toronto to erect a suicide barrier on the Bloor Viaduct.

"I wish Al could see the significant advances in the almost twenty years since his death," says McCamus. "The huge increase in public awareness of mental health causes, the improvements in medications and treatments, the growth of volunteerism and activism, the sensitivity and respect that mental illness issues and suicide prevention initiatives receive in media attention. These were all causes that he cherished and championed as a volunteer at the Schizophrenia Society."

There are no longer suicides at the Bloor Viaduct and, as predicted, no meaningful increase in deaths at other Toronto bridges. The Luminous Veil, now twenty years old, was a practical and aesthetic success, although in recent years the City of Toronto has allowed one of its signature design elements — the ever-changing lights — to fall into shoddy disrepair.

In a bold and important development for suicide prevention, in late 2023 Canada was scheduled to launch a three-digit number, 988, that anyone in need of immediate mental health crisis and suicide prevention intervention could call or text twenty-four hours a day, seven days a week.

The three-digit number will replace the ten-digit crisis hotline that the Canada Suicide Prevention Service began to offer in 2017, as did other organizations across the country. "Research shows these crisis services decrease distress in callers and prevent suicide in the short term," the *Canadian Medical Association Journal* (CMAJ) reported in January 2021. "It's one of the most effective ways we have to intervene in a very high-risk population," Dr. Allison Crawford, chief medical officer for the service, told the *CMAJ*.

Bill Pringle, a Saskatoon man who had attempted suicide eight times, told the *CMAJ* that long 1-800 numbers can pose a barrier to access. "A person in the throes of a mental health crisis is not going to remember a 10-digit number. It just isn't going to happen," he said.

Canada's 988 initiative comes a few years after the U.S. did the same. In July 2020, the U.S. Federal Communications Commission adopted rules to establish 988 in all fifty states and five territories.

The three-digit number had an immediate and noteworthy effect in the U.S. In September 2020, CNN reported that "calls to the lifeline increased 45% compared with the same time last year, and the majority of those calls were connected to a counselor, according to the U.S. Department of Health and Human Services."

The data, CNN said, "shows that in August [2020], a total of 361,140 calls, chats and texts were routed to a 988-lifeline call center. Among them, 84% of calls, 97% of chats and 98% of texts were answered and engaged by a counselor — representing a total of about 88% of people who reached out to the lifeline."

"The three-digit number is a great idea," says McCamus. "It seems to be needed now more than ever."

Indeed, it does. The factor that drives most people to kill themselves — mental illness — seems to be a greater problem than it was in 1997, when Birney and McCamus began their campaign. In March 2023, the *New York Times* reported "record levels of sadness in the most recent Youth Risk Behavior Survey conducted by the Centers for Disease Control and Prevention. According to the recently released survey, which was given to 17,000 adolescents at high schools across the United States in the fall of 2021, nearly three in five teenage girls felt persistent sadness in 2021, double the rate of boys, and one in three girls seriously considered attempting suicide. The data also showed high levels of violence, depression and suicidal thoughts among lesbian, gay and bisexual youth."

It is likely that a similar survey conducted in Canada would elicit comparable results.

The Luminous Veil (date unknown).

Canadian adults are also experiencing an increase in suicidal thoughts. "The prevalence of suicidal ideation since the pandemic began was 4.2%, which was significantly higher than the pre-pandemic prevalence of 2.7% in 2019," a May 2022 Statistics Canada study concluded. "A statistically significant increase in prevalence was observed among females and males, age groups younger than 65, and several other sociodemographic groups."

Another disconcerting story that sounded all too familiar to the Bloor Viaduct barrier advocates concerned the plan to install safety nets on the Golden Gate Bridge, North America's number one suicide magnet.

In 2008, bridge officials had voted to "move forward with the net, meant to deter those looking to jump to their deaths and catch those who do," Associated Press (AP) reported in late November 2022.

Work on the net began in 2018 and was set to be completed by January 2021, but it has been repeatedly delayed. "The project aims to add 20-foot-wide (6 metres) stainless steel mesh nets on both sides of the 1.7-mile (2.7 kilometre) bridge and replace maintenance platforms used by bridge workers that were built in the 1950s," AP said.

In late November 2021, two companies — Shimmick Construction and Danny's Construction — filed allegations in state court claiming "that changes to and flaws in the government's net design and the lack of transparency about the deterioration of the bridge's maintenance platforms have raised the construction price from $142 million to at least $398 million," AP reported.

Only about 50 percent of the work had been completed as of late 2022, with a final date projected for December 2023, nearly four years behind schedule.

Optimism

Despite the recent increase in mental health concerns in Canada (and the U.S.) — especially among young people — Michael McCamus says he's optimistic that Canada has turned the corner when it comes to dealing upfront with topics such as suicide, which was once a taboo.

"Stories like that of Jennifer Hicks, where a 'means restriction' strategy likely saved her life, show there are actions we can take to help the approximately two hundred people who, according to the Public Health Agency of Canada, contemplate or attempt suicide every day."

He also lauds those who want to talk about suicide, not pretend the problem doesn't exist. "We have to deal with suicide head-on and in public," he says, "but in a way that doesn't trigger vulnerable people to take their own life."

Twenty years after the suicide barrier on the Bloor Viaduct became a reality, McCamus sees the Veil as just one part of a large mental health movement sweeping across Canada that has resulted from increased public awareness and public support for mental health initiatives.

"What I learned from this experience is that no problem is too big to tackle, whether it's mental health advocacy, gun violence, climate change, whatever," he says. "The solutions are not beyond the reach of ordinary people working together with a common cause in a free and democratic country like Canada.

"When Al Birney started talking about the viaduct problem in 1997, he was alone, completely alone. City Hall seemed like an unmovable object. But month-by-month, year-by-year, Al found people who shared a stake in solving the problem: bereaved families, police, firefighters, psychiatrists, crisis workers, history buffs, and local politicians. Our little team of volunteers pooled our efforts and, with a lot of determination, and a little luck, we became an unstoppable force. We fought City Hall and we won, and if we can do that — plain, ordinary folks — anyone can do it. And that gives me great hope for the future."

Acknowledgements

This book would never have existed without Michael McCamus. He suggested the idea, provided endless access to his detailed files, and offered invaluable feedback on my drafts. His assistance was provided without complaint, often late into the night after a long day teaching in Vietnam (where he now lives).

I know he would also want to acknowledge the incredible contribution of the late Al Birney, who, along with Michael, fought for more than four years to convince city hall to erect a suicide barrier on the viaduct. These two ordinary citizens, along with other volunteers, showed what passionate determination and endless hard work can accomplish.

My thanks to Russell Smith, my excellent and supportive editor at Dundurn Press, to Elena Radic, Dundurn's amazing managing editor, and to Jeremy Lucyk, my editor at Centennial College Press, who opened the door for me at Dundurn.

I am also indebted to the many people who agreed to talk to me for the book, often about painful memories. And to my family and friends for understanding that I had to write most days for about a year, rather than spend time with them.

I also want to acknowledge the powerful book, *Gardens of Shame: The Tragedy of Martin Kruze and the Sexual Abuse at Maple Leaf Gardens*, by Cathy Vine and Paul Challen. It provided invaluable information about Martin and the longtime pedophile ring that operated at MLG.

Lastly, I want to say that if this book, like the Luminous Veil, influences even one person not to take their life, then all the hard work will have been well worth it.

If You Need Help

This book contains detailed descriptions of people's experiences with mental illness, psychosis, suicide, murder-suicide, and child sexual abuse, taken from news media reports and the author's interviews with survivors and their families and supporters.

If you or someone you know is struggling with mental health, addiction, or sexual abuse, help is available. The participants of this book, including survivors, families, and mental health professionals all agree: Hope is an option. Recovery is not only possible, it is probable. Talk to someone. Speak with your family doctor or local hospital. Ask for help.

In Canada, a new three-digit number to reach a mental health hotline will be launched in late 2023: **Call 988** if you or someone you know needs assistance. The same 988 number already exists in the United States. Until it is in place in Canada, call the helpline at: **1-833-456-4566**.

Image Credits

Index

About the Author

 Paul McLaughlin is an award-winning freelance writer, broadcaster, and author of about a dozen books (many private commissions), hundreds of magazine and newspaper articles, and countless broadcast scripts. A leading interviewing expert, he has written two books on how to interview, the most recent being *Asking the Best Questions: A Comprehensive Interviewing Handbook for Journalists, Podcasters, Bloggers, Vloggers, Influencers, and Anyone Who Asks Questions Under Pressure.* A former interviewing and performance trainer for CBC Radio and TV, Paul has taught journalism and professional writing since 1978 and currently teaches at York University. As well as being a professional playwright, he has also spent many years as a communications consultant for Kroll Lindquist Avey, one of the world's leading forensic and investigative accounting firms. His website is paulmclaughlin.ca.